TØ168868

I highly recommend it for anyone wrestling with self-acceptance and appearance diversity, and especially for parents who want reassurance and comfort when making major medical choices for their child. This book is not a how-to manual for life, but rather a how-I'm-doing-it, heart-to-heart conversation that will stick with you long after you finish the story. Kristin is a role model not just for other children and teens with craniofacial differences, but truly for anyone who wants to pursue a life committed to self-reliance, continual improvement, and personal resolve.

—ERICA MOSSHOLDER, executive director,
Children's Craniofacial Association

DIARY OF A BEAUTIFUL DISASTER

Kristin Bartzokis

KiCam
PROJECTS

Cover and book design by Mark Sullivan

ISBN 978-0-9977222-3-9

Published by KiCam Projects
Georgetown, Ohio
www.KiCamProjects.com

Printed in the United States of America.
Printed on acid-free paper.

This book is dedicated to all those affected by craniofacial anomalies. Know you are never alone. So many of us are fighting a similar fight. Stay strong and choose to be positive. It makes all the difference.

* * *

To the medical staff involved in our reconstructive processes: Thank you for choosing this career path. You work tirelessly to bring a sense of normalcy to our lives.

* * *

A special thanks goes to my reconstructive surgeon, Dr. S. Anthony Wolfe. Your knowledge, skill, and dedication have impacted my life from the first moment my parents brought me to your office. I am forever grateful for every decision we made together.

* * *

Preface

These pages tell the story of my life, the life of a woman in her early thirties who is afflicted with an unusual facial anomaly known as Treacher Collins syndrome. In deciding how best to tell my story, I felt a simple narrative approach would not properly convey the emotions I experienced as I dealt with various obstacles in my life. Though the narrative form worked well to tell the basic story of how I grew into the person I am today, it seemed inadequate to detail the most traumatic incidents of my life: my numerous craniofacial surgeries. To share my emotions surrounding those procedures, I needed a different approach, something more visceral, so I chose to relate the stories of my surgeries as journal entries. Those "entries" do not come verbatim from a diary, but from my recollections, the recollections of my parents, actual notes and letters written by my parents at the time of my surgeries, and medical records provided by my doctor.

These chapters create a more intimate, emotional understanding of those trying times. It's one thing to read about an experience; it's another to live in that very moment.

I interspersed journal entries from my perspective as well as from the vantage points of my mother, Pat, and my father, Chris. My parents have memories of surgeries I was too young to recall, and it was important to me to show how syndromes like mine affect the entire family, not just the patient.

Reliving certain moments was often difficult for me and for my parents, but I wanted to hold nothing back. What appears in the pages that follow is the unvarnished truth about my life.

Prologue: Disaster Strikes

Shortly before nine at night on December 28, 1982, a young man left Broward General Hospital in Fort Lauderdale, Florida, and headed toward his law office in Miami to pick up a file he needed for a trial the next day. His mind was neither on work nor the road. Instead, he focused on his wife and their baby, born seven hours earlier. Something was wrong with the baby. Her ears were underdeveloped, and she had other apparent facial anomalies. At first, he'd tried to shrug off the baby's unusual appearance as simply swelling from the birthing process; however, deep inside he sensed something else was wrong. As he made his way down I-95, he was so lost in thought that he failed to notice that there was no other traffic on the highway. His was the only car traveling in either direction as he approached the downtown area.

When he reached his destination, he parked his car in the lot adjacent to his office building across from the county courthouse. He then made his way inside the office building and up to his fifth-floor suite, where he picked up the file he needed and then checked his phone messages. When he was finished, he took the elevator back down to the lobby and exited the building toward his car. As he stepped outside, however, he noticed something strange: the smell of smoke. He looked around to see what might be burning, but he saw nothing. Then he noticed something even stranger; there was no movement anywhere around him, no other cars or people in the vicinity of the courthouse. He had never seen anything like that before, especially in this part of the city. There was always someone around, always something happening. He wondered why everything seemed so eerie.

The young man drove his car away from the parking lot toward the ramp that led to I-95 North. In a few moments, he was on the highway; however, something caught his attention very quickly. For the first time that night he noticed there were no other cars on the road. Plus, the smell of smoke was getting stronger. "What in the world is going on?" he thought to himself. "This feels like a *Twilight Zone* episode." He decided to turn on the radio to see if he might learn something on the news, and within moments he had his answer.

"The rioting has spread from Overtown into Liberty City," the commentator said, "and police are warning all citizens in the area not to leave their homes. Stay off State Road 7 and I-95 and any other roadways in the immediate vicinity."

"Oh my God!" the young man cried out to himself. He was driving right through the danger zone, the precise area police had just warned people to avoid. He looked around and saw that his was still the only car on the highway. Plumes of smoke appeared to his left and to his right. The glow of flames shone in the distance. The young man was terrified. He thought back to two years earlier when violence and destruction erupted in the same part of the city. Three unsuspecting young men, returning home from a fishing trip, drove their car right into the center of the violence. They were forced to stop, dragged from their car, and savagely beaten to death by a volatile mob.

As he drove north on the highway, the young man feared he would find himself in the same circumstance of being in the wrong place at the wrong time. Would there be a mob blocking his path ahead? If so, what would he do? Would he accelerate and try to drive through them? Would he stop and hope for mercy from the crowd? Should he turn around and try his luck the other way? He simply didn't know which option offered the best chance for his survival. So he kept driving and hoped he would make it back to his wife and daughter.

By now the young man was running on adrenaline. He drove as fast as his small car could handle, reaching 110 miles per hour. He prayed to see a police officer—the first time in his life he had wanted to be pulled over for speeding. None was to be found. As he approached every rise, he looked ahead to see if there might be an angry mob stretched across the road, but each time he did, he saw none. As he continued traveling north, he began to believe he might actually survive the night. Finally, he arrived at the Golden Glades Interchange, a major intersection of highways that provides multiple avenues of escape in several directions, and for the first time since leaving Miami, he felt he was safe. His ordeal was over. He hoped the same would be true for the people who were still caught up in the mass violence he had just escaped.

Fortunately, the city of Miami survived the danger that night, and the young man who made that perilous trip into the city continues to enjoy life with his family.

* * *

I'm glad about that, because that man is my father. And as you might have guessed by now, the reason my father was so distraught that night was because of me. Yes, I'm the girl with the malformed ears and the other facial abnormalities that my father worried so much about. You might wonder what happened to me after that night? Well, I survived too. And I have done pretty well in my life. I have dealt with some very difficult moments, but I also have experienced moments of pure joy.

I was born on a day a terrible disaster rocked the Miami area. Fortunately, the catastrophic consequences of some disasters can be overcome. My life is a testament to that. It would have been easy for me to give up on myself, to say I didn't belong in a world of normal-looking people. But I didn't do that. Instead I persevered; I fought to overcome my innate disadvantages. Along the way I suffered a lot, but I also laughed a lot. I lost some battles, but I also won many. In the end, I became stronger from my experiences. I learned that I matter, both to myself and to others. I also learned that I should be proud of who I am, and who I might someday become.

So, although I might have entered my life in the middle of a disaster, and though my own life might have had moments of disaster along the way, the ensuing years have been rewarding. That's why I like to think of my life as one continuing adventure; one continuing disaster, if you will. But a beautiful disaster at that.

This is my story.

December 1982: And So It Began

My name is Kristin. Some people call me Kris, KB, Bart, or the girl who can do no-handed cartwheels. After all, I was a champion gymnast. Unfortunately, I was born with a facial deformity, a problem that seems to define the person I am no matter what else I might accomplish in life.

Growing up, I believed that everything happened for a reason. God gave people only what He knew they could handle. The strong were given seemingly insurmountable challenges because He knew they could overcome them. I clung to those beliefs for as long as I could; I had to in order to stay sane through years of hospital visits. Eventually, my opinions changed, and I came to believe that life consisted of moments of chance, coincidence, and pure luck. I adopted a more cynical, realistic view of life, one that held that there was no such thing as fate or destiny. My craniofacial abnormality came from a random genetic mutation, plain and simple. It wasn't written in the stars. It wasn't given to me by God as a test of strength, knowing that if anyone could handle the problem, it would be me. It could've been you instead of me. Maybe you would've handled it differently. Who knows?

Over the years, I've done everything I could to prevent people from thinking of me as the girl with the funny face. I wanted them to think of me instead as the great gymnast, the great soccer player, or the straight-A student. Sometimes I was successful; sometimes I was not. When I was not, it created a great deal of conflict in my life, and that conflict greatly shaped the person I have become. I tend to bottle up everything inside myself, not wanting to show my vulnerabilities, not wanting to reveal who I really am. I even have the ability to change personas, almost on a daily basis, so that people can see me as I think they want to see me, rather than as I actually see myself. I do that because I am afraid that if people truly know me, they will feel sorry for me, treat me with pity, and not think of me as just another acquaintance or another good friend.

As a result of my congenital deformity, it seems as though I have been battling demons all my life, sometimes of my own making. I am certain I have wrongly imagined people mocking me when they were actually laughing about something else. For people like me, that happens quite often; it comes with the territory. If there is laughter around us, we feel it must be directed toward us because we look different or strange. But I have done my best to overcome my insecurities, and I think I have succeeded—at least in part.

I still tend to be reserved, not wanting to reveal to people who I truly am. I still prefer that the world think I am happy all the time, even though I am not. But despite my tendency to hide my true feelings from people, I have begun to change my approach to life. I am beginning to open up; I am finally willing to reveal my rawest and most vulnerable self. Perhaps the years have matured me so that I no longer have to run away from who I am. Or perhaps I'm simply tired of trying to be someone I'm not. Whatever the reason, the story that follows will show the real me.

I have to admit this is one of the most difficult things I have ever done, this act of self-awareness, but one that I am proud to tackle. I believe that what people will learn about me as I open up to them is that I am a fighter. I don't back down from challenges—not even when it means revealing my innermost feelings to strangers.

And now it is time for me to face the challenge head-on. One that I have avoided for so many years. I only hope I do it well.

Many would call me hard or stoic. I would agree with them. I have worked tirelessly over the years to learn how to not cry, how to control my emotions, how to never expose my heart. I felt that if I didn't learn to be tough, I would become overwhelmed by my problems. I therefore have no one to blame or credit for my tough emotional makeup but myself. In a very great sense, however, my toughness might be my downfall. If I don't let people in because I'm afraid I might get hurt, I might be shutting out people who can truly help me.

I'd like to tell you I handled my facial anomaly unassertively, but that has not always been true. Instead, I often charged through life aggressively and with a purpose, fueled by my desire to deal with my abnormalities head-on. Though at times my sole wish was to blend in with my peers, I realized at a young age that I could control how other people viewed me. If I didn't want them to focus on my facial deformities, I would need to command respect. The best way to do that would be to emphasize that my flawed appearance did not limit my physical, mental, and athletic abilities.

Still, no matter how much I tried to impress people with my athletic achievements, I wondered how they actually viewed me. I could control the image I projected, but I could not control their wandering minds. I remember learning about fetal alcohol syndrome in my high school biology class and wondering how many of my classmates made assumptions about my physical appearance. Fetal alcohol syndrome causes facial abnormalities such as small eyes and flattened cheekbones. At first glance, one might think I had it. Very few people ever asked about my facial structure, and unless prompted, I never spoke of it. I later learned that many of my classmates assumed I was badly burnt in a fire.

But my scars were not due to a car accident or a fiery blast. I was born with Treacher Collins syndrome, a rare facial anomaly caused by mutated genes. It affects the growth of the facial structure and varies across a wide spectrum of severity. I have undergone countless surgeries to repair my underdeveloped facial bones, and I consider myself lucky to have a case that is repairable. Patients with the most severe cases require trachea and feeding tubes to help them breathe and eat, and some have such a large percentage of their facial bones missing that their features are shapeless.

My case is moderate. I exhibit the traits commonly associated with TCS: underdeveloped chin and cheekbones, recessed jaw, downward-slanting eyes, and malformed ears. I wear a bone-conduction hearing aid across my head like a headband. My tiny, misshapen ears do not allow me to place a hearing aid in or behind them. When I was born, I had a cleft palate, a hole in the roof of my mouth that made eating a daily challenge. My nasal passage is narrow, as is my trachea, making for somewhat nasally speech and problematic nighttime breathing. I spent the first ten years of my life in speech therapy to ensure I properly used my voice rather than relying on lip reading or sign language.

I let these characteristics define only a part of me. Perhaps others would expect me to say that I don't let my syndrome define me at all, but that would be a lie. If my syndrome didn't somehow affect me, I wouldn't be human. Nor would I have a story to tell. My flaws make me noticeable, but my strength makes me memorable.

* * *

My story began on December 28, 1982, in Fort Lauderdale, Florida. I was born to two excited twenty-eight-year-olds who thought they were having a perfectly healthy baby girl.

After I stubbornly entered the world, the doctor announced "It's a girl" with trepidation in his voice. He held me up to give my parents a quick glance at their newborn baby, as every doctor does, but before they had time to look closely, the nurses scurried out of the room with me.

My parents didn't notice anything unusual about their tiny infant with a swollen face and cone-shaped head. She seemed perfectly normal. Besides, I was their first child, and they didn't know what to expect, especially after an intense labor like my mother had just had.

The nurses went about their business without acknowledging I had a problem, but their actions grew tense. My dad quietly grew suspicious of their anxious mannerisms. Minutes later, the doctor emerged to ask about any family history of ear problems. From what he could tell, I had abnormally small, malformed ears. It wasn't until the post-birth swelling abated that my lack of facial bone structure and cleft palate came into focus. Then it all became clear; I had a problem. The nurses avoided my family because none of the hospital staff seemed to know how to relate to the parents of an imperfect infant.

While still in the hospital, I underwent various tests. My underdeveloped facial features triggered concerns that other parts of my body also might not have fully developed. Doctors performed an ultrasound on my kidneys because they grow at the same rate as the facial bones. The test revealed nothing unusual. We left the hospital without my parents having any answers.

A few weeks later, my pediatrician ordered a series of hearing tests, and from what he read in the chart, the ear, nose, and throat doctor reported that I had total deafness. For whatever reason, though, my pediatrician did not fully agree with the initial conclusion and urged my parents to travel to Miami so I could have a brain stem scan. This scan would prove whether I heard any sounds at all. My parents obliged, and as it turned out, the brain stem scan affirmed that I could hear at a certain decibel level. The audiologists who performed the exam couldn't hide their enthusiasm when my infant brain registered sound. I wasn't completely deaf, just hearing impaired. I would require a hearing aid to function, but sound would be a part of my life.

With one mystery solved, there still seemed to be a hundred more questions. The next logical step was to find a doctor to correct my cleft palate. A radiologist who worked with my mom, a radiation therapist herself, suggested a nearby surgeon. He had recently written a book on cleft palate reconstruction and seemed to be our best hope. My parents immediately made an appointment to see him.

This particular surgeon did not have the best bedside manner, and when he realized my issues involved more than just a cleft palate, which was all he was trained to handle, he proclaimed, "I can't help you! This is a job for Tony Wolfe." Because I had a number of health issues, I needed help from someone who had in-depth training in craniofacial syndromes. Dr. S. Anthony Wolfe was a world-renowned reconstructive surgeon located in Miami. He specialized in extensive craniofacial repairs, and he would be able to offer my family guidance with my case of multiple facial abnormalities.

It wasn't until my parents connected with Dr. Wolfe that they delved into the underlying cause of my malformed ears, underdeveloped cheekbones, and cleft palate. With a certainty my parents had not yet witnessed about my condition, Dr. Wolfe declared that I had Treacher Collins syndrome. Those three words sent my dad to a medical school library to research the condition that would change all of our lives forever.

Treacher Collins syndrome affects roughly one in 50,000 people, making it one of the more rare genetic disorders. It does not affect mental development or shorten life expectancy, but it does promise to take its patients down the tumultuous path of multiple surgical procedures. Reconstructive surgeons perform these operations on an as-needed basis and at certain times in patients' lives. This is because facial bones continue to develop as a person grows, and certain procedures need to be performed around specific ages.

Through his research, my father learned that Treacher Collins could be hereditary. In 1982, expectant parents couldn't test their unborn child for TCS. Parents themselves could be tested to see whether they carried the gene, but because the syndrome was relatively rare, testing for the gene wasn't common practice. Regardless, had my parents been tested prior to my birth, absolutely nothing would have been found. Like most genetic diseases, TCS can be hereditary, but it can also be caused by a random gene mutation. Random mutation is an utterly unpredictable occurrence and can strike anyone, as it did in my case.

My parents finally had answers to the biggest mystery to hit their young married life together.

They now had an extremely difficult decision to make. Would they put my fate in the hands of a world-renowned surgeon, or would they spare me the surgeries and allow me to walk through life without making any changes to my appearance? Technically speaking, my symptoms were merely aesthetic. Aside from my cleft palate, the deformities I displayed were not life-threatening. My lack of cheekbones and recessed chin had no effect on my ability to breathe or eventually walk or talk.

On the other hand, the hole in the roof of my mouth needed to be corrected so I could eat properly. As a newborn, I lacked the ability to suck, making breastfeeding impossible and bottle-feeding a chore. My mom would have to squeeze the bottled milk into my mouth in order for me to drink, and even then, I barely wanted to eat. When I moved on to solid foods, I ate small amounts at a time and someone always had to keep a watchful eye over me to ensure food did not lodge itself into my cleft palate. In order to grow at the normal rate, I needed to eat properly, and it became evident that my cleft palate would need correction.

At the age of eighteen months, I sat in the waiting room of Miami Children's Hospital for the first time. The scheduled operation would serve two purposes. The first was to find out whether I could even be intubated. (My surgeon thought my naturally narrow trachea might be too tight.) The second purpose was to close my cleft palate.

After several failed attempts at intubation, the anesthesiologist tried using an uncommon method to sedate me: a fiber optic scope. This is sometimes the only option for people with narrow airways. It proved successful, and within a half hour my surgeon had closed the hole in the roof of my mouth.

My parents now had more options. Because I could be intubated, I could have more surgeries. As a result, I wouldn't be forced to live life with anomalous facial features. My problems could be corrected, at least partially. My parents held the choice in their hands. But could they stand to watch their daughter go through countless operations? What if something happened? Was it *really* necessary? What about the pain I might feel and the residual scarring? But if they didn't act, what kind of life would I live? Would I have friends? Would I be teased ceaselessly? Would I be able to live a normal life? Would the emotional scars from not building up my facial bones be more of a burden than the physical scars from surgery?

After weighing all plausible scenarios, the answer became clear. Providing their child with the best possible life meant taking action: action toward self-confidence, action toward a normal life, and action against bullying. From the moment of that decision, multiple reconstructive surgeries filled my formative years.

AUGUST 23, 1984 | *Pat:*

Back in April, the cleft palate clinic gave us the all clear for Kristin to have her cleft palate corrected. Since then, I've enjoyed watching her grow and learn, but all the while, I've suppressed my anxiety toward this very day. The moment of truth has arrived. It's finally time for her first surgery.

Last night, we checked Kristin into Miami Children's Hospital in Coral Gables, Florida. While undergoing the pre-admission process, we learned that her surgery start time was pushed from 8 a.m. to 2 p.m. That's a six-hour delay! For an eighteen-month-old, that's an eternity, especially when all food consumption ceased at midnight. Luckily, she was able to continue sipping apple juice until 8 a.m.

The anxiety caused by the lengthy wait frustrated us. We wandered the halls, pushing Kristin in her brown stroller for hours on end. Her little feet kicked up and down as she took in the sights of the sterile environment. She was hungry, thirsty, and asking for juice, but didn't understand why we were holding out on her. As it is, she eats like a bird, and now when she actually wanted food, we could not provide it. We were heartbroken. We felt as if we turned our backs on our daughter in her time of need.

We continued to wait, but our patience dwindled. Dr. Wolfe's first surgery of the day had experienced complications, forcing the waiting game to continue even longer. Kristin's surgery would have taken forty-five minutes at the most; she should have had the earliest appointment since it was a simple case. Instead, a seven-year-old boy with Crouzon syndrome marked not only the first operation of the day but also the longest, at seven hours.

Kristin became extremely irritated from fatigue and hunger and wailed like we'd never heard before. She had never been the baby who fussed or caused a scene, only crying when absolutely necessary. Seeing her react this way, I lost my temper. Neither her father nor I could stand seeing how this process tore her apart. I begged to be able to feed her a few sips of milk, just to ease her discomfort. When the administration refused, we almost walked out of the hospital not planning to return that day, but we didn't because Kristin cried herself to sleep right then and there. After Kristin's brief nap, the nurses woke her for a shot of calming medicine. Then, ten minutes later, they wheeled her away from us and toward the surgical unit. It's possible they moved her prematurely because they saw all of us growing increasingly agitated. We suspect she waited in the pre-op area for an extensive amount of time before being brought into surgery. Either way, at least now she was calm, resting, and not focusing on her hunger.

This was the first time I ever saw my husband cry. Not many circumstances transformed him to mush, but upon watching his daughter venture toward her first procedure, he willingly let the tears fall. From comforting my unsuspecting daughter, I shifted to soothing my heartbroken husband.

Waiting continued to be the name of the game. Kristin's own surgery lasted longer than anticipated. The nurse assigned to our hospital room saw the anxiety in our eyes and ventured down to the operating room for a progress report: The surgery was almost complete and everything went well. Those were the most beautiful words anyone had ever spoken to me. Everything. Went. Well.

The previous twenty-four hours were the most stressful I'd ever encountered. I simply wanted my daughter to return to her hospital room. Eventually, Dr. Wolfe came to talk to us. Originally, he questioned whether he would be able to intubate her because of her narrow trachea. While it took time, the intubation was a success and the actual surgery to close the hole in her soft palate lasted a brief fifteen minutes. He mentioned there might be a need in the future for more surgery to extend her palate back, but that would happen in due time. If done, this would correct any possible speech impediments she might face because of her syndrome.

Though the entire day seemed drawn out and overly emotion-filled, I couldn't complain. After all, the surgery was successful. We witnessed support from all the other parents there that day. We shared the bond of feeling utterly helpless for our children's situations. I felt like I'd known each of these parents for a very long time, but I knew this bond was temporary. When we left, only the memory of the loss of control we felt remained.

Kristin finally rejoined us in her room. Her father was all too eager to scoop her up in his arms. And with nothing but love in his eyes, he again cried as he held her. Kristin's nose and mouth were bloodied, and the IV tube remained in her arm, but she was comforted by being back in our presence. Traces of the medication from surgery still flowed through her body as she lay there relaxing. I knew she would sleep soundly that night. Wouldn't we all.

* * *

AUGUST 24, 1984 | *Pat:*

Kristin slept for nineteen hours straight! Yesterday really took a toll on her tiny body. Her cheerful disposition returned today, but she hasn't been very talkative. The nurses removed her IV tube today and we tried force-feeding her more fluids through a bottle. With the procedure done to the roof of her mouth, swallowing hurt and she refused to drink much. We did however successfully spoon-feed her a little orange sherbet, her favorite! I'm sure the frozen treat soothed the irritated area, but that didn't change the fact that she wouldn't drink liquids. The lack of fluids caused her to run a slight fever, so Dr. Wolfe requested she spend another night in the hospital.

* * *

AUGUST 25, 1984 | *Pat:*

Today we brought Kristin home from the hospital. We're all overjoyed to be home, but the recovery doesn't cease just because we changed environments. Dr. Wolfe placed Kristin on a diet consisting solely of soft food until he sees her in his office for a follow-up visit. We followed his instructions even when she cried watching us eat sandwiches. Soon enough she'll be back to eating what we eat, but for now, we need to focus on recovery.

Overall, Kristin handled this whole experience as well as possible, though we noticed one residual effect; she now needs to be reassured of our close proximity while she falls asleep at night. I'm sure this will pass, but I'm coming to understand that even at a young age, kids recognize distress. In due time, life will return to normal. Until then, we will continue to affirm our presence in her life.

Growing Up Ordinary

From the moment my parents realized I would have a difficult life ahead of me, they vowed to do everything in their power to ensure my day-to-day life would be as ordinary as possible. They didn't know the details of what I would face over the years, whether my future operations would break me, or if I'd be at the receiving end of cruel remarks from my peers, but they knew they had to raise me to believe I could accomplish anything. They instilled in me an unlimited outlook on life, which allowed me to forget about my syndrome and focus on all the ways that I was similar to my peers, rather than how I was different.

The fact that I had a syndrome did not cause my parents to shelter me or hold me back from doing things other children did. From the very beginning, they raised me to understand my limitations: no swimming while wearing my hearing aid and no horseplay after a surgery. Other than that, I never heard the phrases *you can't, you won't,* or *you'll never.* I could accomplish anything as long as I put forth the effort. With that upbringing, I gained the confidence to explore a variety of activities without worrying that my disability might be a hindrance. In my mind, I had no disability when it came to confronting challenges. I was just like anybody else.

My parents knew they had to deal with the negatives in my life, but they didn't have to dwell on them. They treated my problems as mere inconveniences rather than as major obstacles. More importantly, they took great pains to impart that attitude to me, and to this day that is how I live my life. I thrived because my parents gave me the chance to live a full and happy life. I'm convinced that this unlimited outlook is the most important reason for my success. It allowed me to remain positive during the hard times.

I'm grateful when people tell me they are impressed by the kind of person I have become. This validates the way I live my life. I don't let much bother me, and I take everything life throws at me in stride. The way I see things, there's only one way for me to deal with my difficulties: with acceptance. I did not ask for a life with problems. I never wanted to deal with the emotional scarring and physical pain associated with my disability, nor would I ever wish that kind of life on anyone else. Nevertheless, I have learned to deal with my anomalies as best I can.

Many people complain about the hand they've been dealt in life. They harbor ill will toward others who are more fortunate and they are wary of the world around them, often waiting to pounce on the next unsuspecting person who might offend them in some way, real or imagined.

I refuse to live this way. My condition is no one's fault. It's not a curse or prison sentence; it's a way of life. Holding a grudge against the world would do nothing to improve my situation, so I refuse to entertain any thoughts along those lines. Of course, I have my difficult moments, but I steady myself and move on. Dwelling on the unchangeable will not reverse my situation. I owe this mentality to my parents, because they always found a way to help me assimilate to my surroundings.

From birth I was taught to believe that my life was limitless. When I was sixteen weeks old, my parents enrolled me in the Fort Lauderdale Oral School. Even though I was still an infant, they felt I should begin the long process of dealing with my syndrome. I had a hearing impairment and needed to learn how to differentiate between sounds.

I received my first hearing aid when I was six weeks old, which meant that right away my young mind was actively listening to the formation of words and utterances, just like normal-hearing children did. Even if I was nowhere near ready to speak, the sooner I concentrated on using my ears, the more I would rely on their functionality. Because of this, my speech therapist encouraged my mom to cover her mouth when she spoke. I would be forced to hear the words instead of learning to read lips.

Every step my parents took in my development exposed me to a more fulfilling and independent life. But even with that, there were limitations they realized they could not exceed. As amazing as it would have been for me to learn how to speak Greek with my extended family, the way my father did, the speech therapist urged my parents to teach me only one language. My young mind needed to focus on understanding and perfecting English above all else. Also, learning sign language was not an option. The goal was for me to hear independently and not rely on other methods of communication.

By following the therapist's instructions, my parents eliminated a crutch I could have used as I grew older. Though I now wish I could both speak Greek and respond to those who sign to me, I'm thankful for the strict emphasis my therapist placed on learning only one language. It forced me to learn to listen.

I spent ten years in speech therapy. In the beginning, certain letters were difficult for me to pronounce because my cleft palate and narrow nasal passages prevented the normal production of sound. To assist me in overcoming this problem, the therapists turned my learning time into playtime. For the letter *P*, they would place a tiny scrap of tissue on their palms. If I pronounced the *P* sound correctly, the tissue would float into the air. If I spoke through my nose, the tissue would not move. Boy, did I want to make that tissue dance! I enjoyed playing these games so much that I never fully realized I was actually working.

In my later years of therapy, I would read books out loud while using a device that measured nasal emission. The end piece of the device rested in one of my nostrils, and whenever I spoke through my nose, a Styrofoam bead in the tube portion of the device rose up and down. My goal would be to read the chapter without making the bead rise unnecessarily. I usually succeeded.

As the years passed, therapy began to bore me. I wanted to play outside with my friends rather than sit at home with the therapist learning how to speak from my diaphragm. I felt alone during speech therapy. Everyone else my age already knew how to speak properly. Why didn't I? But I slogged on and continued with my lessons because I knew it was for the best.

One day, however, I received some great news. With a huge smile on her face, my speech therapist told me she would no longer be coming over to my house for lessons. I had achieved all the goals she once set for me, and her services were no longer needed. After ten years, my lessons were officially over.

So many emotions coursed through me that day. I felt relieved, excited, and accomplished. I had conquered a major challenge in my life. Now I knew how to use my voice properly; now I could communicate clearly with other people. This no doubt would allow me to fit in better in various social settings.

Focusing on what I *could* do gave me a positive outlook on life. By concentrating on what I shared with others, I considered myself an equal instead of an outcast. Sometimes, however, that attitude was tested. On one occasion, when I was four years old and attending mainstream preschool, I sat on the floor of a local theatre waiting for a children's production of a play to start. At one point, a young blond-haired boy seated in front of me turned around and asked me if I was deaf. I blinked a couple of times and then replied hesitantly, "Yes." His question surprised me because my friend, who was seated next to me, and I were talking while we waited for the show to start. The boy in front of us had obviously heard us speaking with each other. He therefore must have known I was able to hear my friend's comments. How else would I have been able to respond to him? So why, I wondered, did the boy think I was deaf? To me, at that young age, I thought the definition of deaf was the complete inability to hear. In my mind, since I could hear, I wasn't deaf.

But at the time I did not feel like debating that point with the inquisitive boy in front of me; I just wanted to be left alone. So I said yes to him when he asked if I was deaf. In truth, though, his inquiry confused me, and made me wonder if maybe there was something wrong with my hearing. Up to that point, I didn't think I had a hearing problem. I felt as though my hearing aid was just an extension of me. And in every other respect, I was just a normal preschooler, who, at the time, was sitting cross-legged on the wooden floor waiting for the fun to start. Now, however, I began to wonder.

Later that night, my mom confirmed to me that people who suffered from deafness could not hear a single thing. That was not the case with me. Though the entryways to my ear canals were covered with skin, I still could hear some small sounds unassisted.

With the help of my hearing aid, however, I could hear everything. This unusual condition caused me to live in an interchangeable world of sound and silence, depending on whether my hearing aid was on or off. Although this didn't bother me very much, it did become annoying at times, particularly when my hearing aid batteries died without warning. Regardless, I was finally able to understand and appreciate my auditory abilities and limitations. I was not deaf, but I did have some form of hearing impairment.

This newfound knowledge was not without its advantages. In fact, it gave me quite a bit of control over my life, especially when I was a young child. There were several occasions when my parents would yell at me for one thing or another. Rather than listen to their ranting, I would simply turn off my hearing aid as they scolded me. From my perspective, if I could not hear them, I could not get into trouble. Immediately, I would notice smirks form across their previously cross faces. They were chuckling about what I had done; they thought I was being funny, and they would laugh at my ingenuity. With the simple turn of an on/off button, I realized I had found a clever way to get out of trouble. Although I did not know it at the time, self-awareness was beginning to take hold of me.

I know it's difficult to believe, but when I was young, I really did feel normal. I understood at an early age that my life was somehow different than most people's. I knew my peers never visited reconstructive surgeons on a regular basis. I knew they didn't plan their summers around operations. And I knew they had more forgiving childhoods than I did. In truth, however, even though I knew I had more problems than most other children, I considered my issues minor. The difficulties that made my life unique never forced me to feel anything but ordinary. I didn't feel special or different or brave.

This was simply my life, and there was nothing very unusual about it. If an obstacle came my way, I dealt with it, just like anybody would. That I had to endure surgical procedures every so often was not extraordinary; it was just a fact of life. I simply had more obstacles to deal with than most children, but I felt like an ordinary girl living an ordinary life, and never saw myself surviving on more courage or strength than any other kid my age.

I felt so ordinary because my parents always let me be a child. They never tried to dissuade me from engaging in activities that concerned them, even when they knew some frightening things about my syndrome that I didn't. Limited airflow is one of the drawbacks of having a narrow nasal passage. Before having surgery on my mandible and maxilla structures (lower and upper jaw), breathing at night would be bothersome, not only to me, but also to anyone around me. I would often snore loudly, and sometimes I would stop breathing temporarily until I woke up gasping for air. My parents never told me how awful I sounded, or how frightened they were that I would stop breathing completely, until after I had an operation that opened up my airway. Despite my problematic nighttime breathing, they still willingly sent me to sleepovers and sleepaway camps. Had I known the severity of my snoring, I probably would have been too ashamed to sleep anywhere but my own room. Rather than fuel my inhibitions, however, they let me live the way other children did.

As the years progressed, my mind-set began to shift. Maybe I was a little different. Though I still considered myself to be equal to my peers and fully capable of achieving my goals, insecurities slowly began to creep into my thoughts. I realized that even though my parents and friends saw me as an ordinary girl, I really wasn't.

The more I noticed other children whispering about me, the more uncomfortable I began to feel in my own skin. As I grew older, I maintained the belief that I could do anything, but I also became more aware of my physical differences. I more often witnessed strangers assessing my facial abnormality. I couldn't deny it any longer. I looked different, and my spirit broke whenever somebody else pointed that out.

One day in middle school, I sat at the mall food court with a friend. A woman came up to us as we ate our Chinese food, looked me straight in the eyes, and proclaimed, "Jesus loves you." Then she disappeared as quickly as she came. She never acknowledged my friend, never said, "Hello" or "Have a nice day." She simply ruined my meal with a solitary phrase. Apparently she felt I needed to know that the Lord still loved me even with my imperfections, which gave me no comfort at all.

Let me say this to anyone who agrees with this woman's actions: Singling someone out because of her uniqueness, even if doing so is well intended, is not an appropriate act. It does not promote self-love and acceptance; instead, it fosters feelings of self-doubt and isolation. Having a stranger single me out in a crowded establishment made me even more aware of my flaws. It was like tunnel vision. When she spoke, it was only she and I in that moment. The world around me had faded to black, and her eyes bore into me.

That occurrence, that single phrase, scarred me. It serves as a reminder that some people will always see me as flawed or damaged. Or perhaps, it's something deeper. Maybe it's a reminder that *I* will always see myself as flawed or damaged.

That woman may have thought her words were somehow intended to help, but in truth, they ruined my day. They made me only more acutely aware that my appearance differed from everyone else's. I was left feeling distraught and hurt. When I hear that phrase now, my heart drops. Twenty years later, it conjures up the same sensitive response I had when I was a child. My inner self wants to leap out of my body and hide in the darkness for days, to suffer in silence because no one else can appreciate how I grieve from the emotional distress caused by those three, small, otherwise benign words. I experience such a feeling of immense isolation whenever I hear them: *Jesus. Loves. You.* A simple smile from the woman would have sufficed. A smile warms my soul. It communicates love and open-mindedness. I would have accepted a smile with open arms.

By the time I reached high school, I had been fully aware of my facial anomaly for years. I still didn't let my awareness hinder my daily activities. I continued to take advantage of every opportunity that presented itself just as I was taught to do. I played soccer with the city league, I joined various clubs at school, and I maintained a high grade-point average; however, I could no longer outrun the feelings of inadequacy building up inside me. Even if I saw myself as ordinary, I recognized that this might not be evident to strangers at first glance.

I volunteered a lot in high school. One year I decided to devote my time to the Special Olympics. I figured this was a large organization, and they would put on an amazing event for the athletes. My grandparents drove me forty-five minutes to the high school where the games were being held. Back then, I often felt a bit anxious around new people and being in new situations. I could never guess how strangers would react to me.

The high school was bustling with activity. I walked up to the information desk to check in for my shift, but before I could utter a single word, the volunteer asked if I was there to participate. I understood and appreciated her misapprehension about my presence there. I hadn't yet undergone the most significant of my facial surgeries. I looked different from other people, so she assumed I must have been a participant. It wasn't malicious. It wasn't meant to offend me. It was simply ignorance in its true form.

Most people don't know how to act when they approach unfamiliar scenarios, or in the case of that woman, unfamiliar syndromes. Had the volunteer simply asked, "How can I help you?" I wouldn't have dreaded the volunteer work I did that day, standing on the sideline of the basketball court my entire shift. I was so terrified that at any given moment someone might pull me onto the court to participate in the game that I forgot the real reason I was there: to help others.

I wish I had enjoyed my time there, but instead I vowed never to return. I felt like I was the sucker at the end of a punch, like my breath had been forced from my lungs. I much preferred to live in the fantasy world where the girl I saw in my dreams mirrored the girl I saw in my reflection. I hated realizing that outsiders didn't see me the same way. My experience with the Special Olympics taught me that, whether warranted or not, I would always feel judged on my looks. But it also reinforced that I had to do everything within my power to make people focus on my accomplishments rather than on my appearance. I had to show the world that my abilities were unlimited. My biggest motivation for success therefore became the desire to break down the barriers erected by others, and my closest ally became my strength.

MARCH 6, 1986 | *Pat:*

Now that we know Kristin can be intubated, the time has arrived for her first major reconstructive surgery. Last month at the playground, another little girl questioned Kristin about her appearance. At three years old, Kristin doesn't realize she looks any different. When we returned home from the playground, I explained to her that she was missing cheekbones, but Dr. Wolfe would start to correct that soon. She accepted what I told her and continued to play with her toys.

A few days ago, we spent the day touring Miami Children's Hospital at an orientation for new patients. They showed us and many other families the layout of the hospital, taught us what to expect come surgery day, and made us feel comfortable with what undoubtedly will be stressful times. Kristin didn't think much of it other than it was entertaining to play with the other kids and the hospital equipment, yet it still made me feel better to see how at ease she was in this environment. It also helped to be able to talk honestly with her about what to expect. She responded enthusiastically, but I know she can't possibly understand the true weight of her predicament.

Now that the day of the surgery has arrived, I have butterflies in my stomach, but Kristin seems to be doing fine. We arrived at the hospital for pre-registration last night and Kristin underwent the normal medical tests done prior to any operation. The nurse had trouble finding the large vein for drawing blood, and Kristin began to cry as he continuously pricked her with the needle. To avert her attention, her dad suggested they count to ten. "1-2-3…" They continued on until the nurse eventually found the vein. It was then the nurse realized the hospital needed a cross match for her blood type in case a transfusion was necessary. I previously had offered to give my own blood for this very reason but had been reassured a transfusion wouldn't be necessary. These days, there are too many cases of diseases transferring through blood transfusions, and it worries me to think about whose blood she might receive. I'd feel much more comfortable giving Kristin my own blood, but it's too late for me to donate now.

Last night Kristin and I slept in a hospital room. I use the term "slept" loosely, since I really didn't sleep at all. The nurses made appearances all night to take more blood and check vitals. At 7:40 a.m., Kristin was taken in for surgery and now the waiting game begins.

I'm a nervous wreck. I've researched this procedure for extra insight on what to expect. While I wish I didn't feel driven to know every gory detail, I cannot feign an unwillingness to learn. I now have a deeper understanding of the risks. Kristin's little brain will be exposed during the craniotomy, and the very nature of that brings tears to my eyes.

* * *

This procedure lasted much longer than anyone anticipated. It left us all physically and mentally drained. The surgery ended seven hours after Kristin was wheeled behind the operating room doors. Dr. Wolfe visited us when Kristin was moved into the recovery room. He looked exhausted from the unexpectedly tedious procedure, and we felt emotionally wrecked from waiting hours beyond the expectation.

He informed us everything went well. Just as in the surgery to repair her cleft palate, the difficult intubation process derailed any scheduled timeline he had. Kristin moved from the recovery room into the intensive care unit where we finally saw her for the first time post-operation. Our poor baby had swollen, stitched eyes and her head was completely bandaged, making her look like she was wearing a roller derby crash helmet.

This first major operation begins a series of steps toward building up the cheekbones. The surgeon made a laceration across the top of Kristin's head where a headband would normally rest. He then rolled the skin forward to access her facial features. Using bone from her skull, he began the process of layering parietal bone where the cheekbones should have been. We learned that this type of surgery would become frequent throughout Kristin's younger years. Over time, the bone tends to settle into its new surrounding and a portion gets absorbed into the body. That's very common. This requires additional cuts of bone to be layered on top of the old. While some will absorb, some will stay, and slowly the cheekbones will form.

Dr. Wolfe also made incisions below Kristin's lower eyelids and shaped the eyes so they drooped less. Because Treacher Collins patients lack cheek structure, the eyelids have no support to keep shape. Though it seems aesthetic, drooping eyelids means Kristin's eyes do not fully close. When eyes fail to close, it becomes impossible for them to retain moisture, leading to severe dryness. If not corrected, this dryness can lead to damaging results.

* * *

MARCH 7, 1986 | *Chris:*

After being placed in the recovery room to wake up from the surgery, Kristin was moved into the ICU yesterday evening. When asked if she felt any pain, she responded with, "My head has an owie." The nurse fully understood all that she had been through and administered more pain medication, alleviating any discomfort.

Kristin called out for her mom and me because she wanted us to hold her. Our hearts ached and we so desperately wished we could have scooped her up to take the fear away. In the ICU, patients must remain in their beds, but even if that weren't the case, Kristin was placed in an oxygen tent for monitoring. She endured an extended, harrowing surgery for a three-year-old and needed assistance returning her body to its normal state. Because I couldn't remove her from the tent, I poked my head into the tent to keep her company. I'd like to think this closeness calmed her nerves.

My saving grace is knowing that Kristin's mother will be by her side night and day throughout all of this. I had to return to work today. I started a new job only three weeks ago, and I fear I've taken too many days off already. Even if I was able to stay, I wouldn't know what to do. Her mother works in medicine and has been helping out the nursing staff wherever possible. They even allowed her to stay by Kristin's side last night in the ICU. This benefits everyone. Kristin isn't able to wear her hearing aid because of the bandages. I don't know how much she can hear, but it isn't a great deal. Her eyes are still swollen shut, so she's lost the sense of sight too. I can't imagine how foreign all of this must feel to her. I'm sure she senses her mother's presence and has taken comfort in knowing she isn't all alone.

I couldn't imagine her being left on her own in this situation. While walking the halls, I noticed the cutest little blond-haired baby standing up in his crib. I found out that the only visitor he receives is the social worker, because he is dying. His parents couldn't deal with death and they left him to live out his remaining days alone and unloved. That would never happen to Kristin. We will always be here when she needs it most.

I'm anxious for five o'clock, when I can burst through the double doors of the office building and begin my journey down to Miami. Luckily, it is Friday and I can spend the entire weekend watching my daughter regain her positive disposition. That is her best quality: the ability to live happily and positively despite her condition. I need her to reclaim that demeanor as quickly as possible. I am strong in every way possible except when it comes to seeing my little girl suffer. We wouldn't have chosen this path of surgical nightmares if a less invasive alternative existed. We could only do what was available to us. I hope and pray that this life doesn't break her. I want nothing more for her than to live a happy life.

* * *

MARCH 10, 1986 | *Chris:*

Kristin was moved into a regular hospital room the day after her surgery because she was healing quickly. She roomed with a six-year-old cerebral palsy patient who just underwent an operation on her legs. This roommate spent much of the days screaming in pain, so when Kristin was well enough, we wheeled her down to the playroom for a change of scenery. While lying on a mat on the floor, she found a mirror. Between the slits of her squinty, swollen eyes, Kristin saw herself for the first time post-operation, pointed, and asked, "What happened?" She didn't recognize herself.

Other parents would be in the playroom with their children and give us looks of pity. Illness serves as a great equalizer, though. One woman who looked as if she had very few comforts in life frequently visited her nephew. She took one look at Kristin and immediately came up to us and said she would pray for her. Even though this woman didn't have much in her own life, she was praying for the health of our daughter.

Kristin truly does look like she has a tough road ahead of her, but the truth is she will leave here to resume a normal life. She will leave here and live. That is the most important thing, isn't it? Some of these children look like little cherubs, the pictures of health, but looks can be deceiving. One little boy seemed to be completely healthy at first glance, but he has a deadly brain tumor. The family will be flying to Canada in hopes of finding a treatment that can save his life. Our daughter looks beaten to a pulp, but she will live.

Then there was the man in a janitor's uniform squatting against the hallway wall. He looked terribly distraught, and I wondered about his story. I later learned that his son was shaken to death by a babysitter. I could imagine a plethora of the emotions he felt: guilt, fear, sadness, and anger. Though at times I wonder, "Why us? Why do we have to live through this agony?" I know I would forever choose our situation over that man's senseless loss.

* * *

MARCH 12, 1986 | *Pat:*

Day by day, Kristin's swelling recedes and she becomes our kid again. Thursday will mark one week since the surgery. The stitches will be removed that day, and Kristin will be discharged afterward. I'm looking forward to going home and getting back to a normal environment, but Kristin wants to stay at the hospital and continue to play in the playroom with the other kids. It's almost as if she has forgotten the operation already. Let's hope she doesn't have any memories of this experience. She'll have to endure an incredible amount more in the future. The less she remembers, the better.

Immediately after my first major facial reconstructive surgery, I developed certain behavioral problems that I had not exhibited earlier; I was afraid to be alone at night, I didn't eat much, and I became very quiet. No doubt the trauma of that event affected me to a degree. But as the days and weeks went by, I became my old self again, and soon I was back to normal. It seemed that even at a very young age I was able to bounce back from adversity.

We all face adversity at one point or another, but for some people that adversity is an ongoing struggle. How we react to our challenges in life defines us. Some people succumb to adversity; others persevere. Even as a young girl, I chose to attack my problems forcefully, head-on. I vowed to turn obstacles that stood in my way into inconveniences I could push aside. To do that, I knew I would need all the strength I could muster, but I was certain I could do it.

Strength became my closest ally, my most revered friend, my lifeline to safety and self-assuredness. With it, I constantly sought ways to break through seemingly impenetrable barriers. Whether mental, emotional, or physical, my strength became my greatest personal attribute. That quality became the best-known part of my personality, one that everyone soon recognized as distinctly me, and one I did not try to hide. Strength became my brand, and it served me well during the most difficult times of my life.

Throughout all of my hospital visits, nurses would comment on my mental toughness as they gazed upon my misshapen, bruised, and battered face. Though most patients in my condition needed morphine to deal with their pain during the recovery process, I refused it on most occasions. I suppose my nurses didn't often encounter a patient, battered beyond belief, who declined morphine the way I did, but that was my choice. However, I didn't refuse pain medicine because I was a masochist; I refused it because I did not want pain to defeat me. Asking for morphine seemed to me to be a sign of weakness, an admission that I couldn't take it, a confirmation that my surgeries were breaking me. I felt that if I couldn't take pain on that occasion, I might be weak on other occasions as well, even outside the hospital setting. I had to stay true to myself. It was the only way I knew to handle my life.

People often have said that my ability to deal with pain makes me appear cold and indifferent at times, that I don't show a lot of emotion. In actuality that is not the case at all; the opposite is true. I hate pain, I am terrified of pain, and I try to avoid pain whenever possible. But what others need to understand is that for people like me, pain, whether physical or emotional, is a way of life. It is an everyday, every-hour, every-minute occurrence. If I let every instance of pain get to me, I'd be in tears all day long. I can't afford to do that, even though sometimes I feel as though I'd like to have a good cry. So the way I deal with pain is to make it my enemy, to fight it, to not let it rule my life. It's not a perfect existence, but it works for me.

Over the years, as more and more people complimented me on my fortitude, my reliance on that trait increased. I clung to it as if my life depended on it. And it did.

To most people who met me, I seemed to navigate through life with ease, unaffected by my syndrome. That's because I exuded confidence. As a child, I made sure I stood up tall, I looked others directly in the eye when I spoke to them, and I never showed any outward signs of distress when other children paid unnecessary attention to me. In fact, when I was out with my friends, I made it a point to appear as though I never noticed the stares of insensitive children when they gaped at me. I looked beyond them rather than at them. In reality, however, those stares bothered me. Every lingering gaze cut through me like a dagger. I wanted to snap my fingers and become invisible so I could make the humiliation stop. But I needed to remain strong and not show my vulnerabilities to my friends if I wanted them to respect me for who I was. I did everything I could to remain stoic and not give in to the emotions I felt.

When I was alone, however, and I caught children staring at my face, I reacted differently. It was always in one of four ways: I would let them stare and simply pretend not to notice; I would stare directly back at them until they averted their gaze; I would lash out with some rude remark; or I would smile. When I pretended not to notice, I made it seem as if I just wasn't paying attention and avoided the situation all together. When I stared directly back at them, I showed them how uncomfortable it felt. When I singled them out with snarky comments such as, "Can I help you?", "Do you have a staring problem?", or "Take a picture. It lasts longer," I admitted that their staring bothered me. But when I smiled, I almost always received a smile in return. It seemed, therefore, that smiling offered me the best approach when dealing with these situations, and yet, on occasion, I responded negatively. It was just so difficult not to get emotional once in a while.

Throughout the years, I have learned how to deal with weaknesses that affected my life. Vulnerabilities could lead to downfalls, and the last thing I wanted was to lose control of my life, especially if it was obvious to others. I know that sounds petty, particularly for someone who has a lot of issues to deal with, but I have always felt it was important to keep my weaknesses hidden from other people. For this reason, I developed a stoic personality. It has served to keep my vulnerabilities hidden from outsiders, my deepest emotions reachable only by me.

My personal battle to succeed in life is mine and no one else's. Stoicism has allowed me to gain control of my life, especially when dealing with callousness from others. I have never been immune to hurtful words or actions. I feel everything deeply, sometimes too deeply. From my perspective, however, if I don't show that I am affected by those insults, then no one will know how much they really hurt. If I hadn't set up these protective barriers around myself at an early age, I would have rendered myself defenseless, making me an easy target for harassment. And so through the years, a protective wall was slowly erected around my heart. I felt all ranges of emotions but never showed them. Even when I wanted to cry—when I should have cried—I kept the hurt bottled up. When necessary, I would simply walk away and find a place where I could be left alone to concentrate on whatever it was that bothered me.

Some people may feel that by not expressing my negative emotions, I'm somehow ignoring my inner turmoil; that by putting on too strong of a front, I'm in fact weak. I think of it this way: I want my hallmark to be my strength and my positivity. When people get to know me, they realize that even in adversity I find a way to persevere. They admire my unbreakable spirit and how ready I am to always face challenges. They're impressed that I don't show my wounded side after everything I've been through. They don't pity me because of my deformity. They respect me for my resilience.

My emotional strength has allowed to me live an ordinary life. But that attitude has been greatly enhanced by another asset I possess, which has done more for my confidence than perhaps anything else that has ever touched me, and that is my athletic ability. More than any other attribute I may possess, I believe it is my physical strength and abilities that have allowed me to live a life with endless possibilities.

When you live life without limitations, you rarely question whether anything can be possible; instead, you take the steps to make things possible. You achieve more because you're open to more. My door to possibility opened the moment I enrolled in gymnastics. I immediately felt drawn to athletics, though at the time I was unaware of the tremendous impact it would have on my life. The more I endured with my operations, the more I focused on becoming a stronger, more powerful athlete. I vowed that my physical strength would become my greatest tool for breaking down stereotypes. Gymnastics sat at the forefront of this mission.

My coaches treated me as equal to my peers right from the start. They would acknowledge my recent surgeries but push me to my limits nonetheless. They recognized my abilities and understood that I wouldn't have been allowed back to practice if my doctor didn't think my body could handle the hard work. When I wanted to slack off during sit-ups, my coaches encouraged me to reach the limit like the rest of the team. If they saw me struggling, they probably would have backed off, but they never had to. I kept up with my teammates because weakness wasn't a good look on me.

My athleticism was one of the ways I obtained the respect I

demanded. It's one of the reasons I led a bully-free life as a child. I was physically more capable than my classmates and made sure they knew it. I always pushed myself to do the most pull-ups during the annual physical fitness tests, even surpassing the boys. I wouldn't stop at the minimum requirement to earn the highest-ranking patch. I had to crush everyone else. Why? Simply because I could. By doing so, I stated a point: Respect me.

My strength commanded attention. I was thought of as the girl to beat, not the girl with a weird face. I was the girl who did "ninjas" (back handsprings), not the girl who had surgeries.

I was Kristin, not Treacher Collins.

Athletics gave me a chance to shine my brightest and prove my greatness. It emphasized strength while nurturing the competitive spirit. It solidly displayed my abilities to anyone watching. I began to crave the physicality of sports. Athletics demanded attention by being visible and tangible, while art and intelligence focused more on quiet, personal goals. Sports always appeared more bois-terous, and that in-your-face, obnoxious attitude was exactly how I planned to be noticed. I needed something physically challenging to overshadow my physical flaws.

When I joined the competition team in gymnastics, I initially offered sub-par performances and won only two ninth-place ribbons throughout the entire season. My parents hadn't real-ized that the summer prior to competition season, I should have been practicing gymnastics. Instead they enrolled me in computer camp with the rest of my school friends.

The following summer, my will to succeed led me to spend every waking hour at the gym. I trained privately with my coaches to perfect my weakest skills and practiced on my own even when I didn't have to. My muscles grew stronger and the skills became easier. I repeated level four, the introductory phase in competitive gymnastics, and effortlessly won most of my competitions, thanks to the excessive training I forced upon my nine-year-old body. During competitions, parents from opposing teams were often overheard discussing the unfair advantage my team gained by having held me back for another year. It seemed I had people right where I wanted them: discussing my superior skills and not my syndrome.

During the final meet of level four, I achieved a victory that was a first in the state of Florida (or so I was told). I received a perfect score, a perfect ten. This meant I had performed my floor routine flawlessly without a single flexed foot, bobble, or bent knee. It's a near impossible feat to be perfect in anything, but I, a girl full of flaws, achieved perfection before anyone else. I tore down any lingering barriers between judgment and reality that day.

Even in that time of tremendous triumph, my stoicism held the reins. As the scoreboard turned toward the audience, a thunderous reaction came from the crowd, drowning out every other sound in the gymnasium. My coach thought the bleachers were caving in, but as the scoreboard turned to face my team, he realized the cause of the crowd's exhilaration. My team saw the perfect score and joined in the commotion as I sat there unfazed. I hugged my coaches and teammates, accepted their congratulations, and continued watching the other competitors as if nothing extraordinary had just happened. I was humbled yet simultaneously aware that I'd always considered perfection attainable. Of course I recognized the improbability, but I never doubted the possibility.

That meet, I won every single event in addition to the all-around title. I didn't even bother returning to my seat in between the award presentations for the individual events. I wasn't arrogant; I was victorious. Being raised without limitations allowed me to push beyond any preconceived notions about a person with a physical anomaly—that I was weak, slow, stupid, or inconsequential. I was none of those things. I was raised to believe I could even defy gravity, and I accepted that challenge. I proved myself that day by winning five gold medals.

My total domination of the competition flattened critics, but the most impressive aspect of the day came with the realization that a girl with a hearing impairment earned a perfect score on the floor exercise, an event synchronized to music. This was the day that gymnasts, coaches, and judges from the state of Florida opened their minds to possibilities. I wasn't to be pitied for my syndrome. Despite wearing a hearing aid, I heard every single beat of the floor music and knew precisely how to execute each move. My perfection garnered lasting respect.

Gymnastics instilled in me a drive that I might not otherwise have known possible. It taught me to find an ally in my physical strength, to fight for what I wanted, and to prove that I have nothing holding me back. From that point forward, I may have been recognized for my face, but I was remembered for my talent.

I continued to navigate through gymnastics with grace, determination, and success. It became an outlet for aggression more than creativity by forcing me to push my body to extremes. To reach success, I had to push harder, fly higher, and run faster. I allowed any negativity to be my motivation, as if it were seeping through my veins and fueling my workouts. As we often heard in practice, pain was just the weakness leaving your body, and my body wanted all of that toxic weakness to spew out of its pores like sweat.

Sometimes I think my coaches forgot just how motivated I was. And like a child too smart for the average class in school, I wouldn't reach my full potential unless someone recognized the need to push me further. The summer when I was twelve years old, the owner of my gym pulled a group of girls together to train with him as the next superstars in the making. I was the only one from my clique not invited into this group, which I found frustrating. Eventually, he included me, but to this day, I'm uncertain why he changed his mind and invited me to join his special group. Maybe he saw my potential; maybe he'd forgotten to include me in the first place; maybe he just felt sorry for leaving me out and invited me out of obligation. I didn't know then, and I'll never know now. I was the first gymnast he ever coached to a perfect score, yet I was the last person who came to mind as the next superstar.

Nonetheless, I spent my summer in daily ten-hour practices. The first four hours were dedicated to my special group for growing, strengthening, and prospering. Each morning, I learned how to become an even more effective gymnast by drawing from my strengths. We focused on endurance and conditioned our bodies to peak form. At the end of the summer, we were judged on our current routines to see just how the practices had affected us. When I performed on the uneven bars, I flawlessly hit moves most people missed. My routine earned a 9.7, a mere three-tenths of a point away from perfect, and the owner of the gym finally acknowledged I indeed belonged in his band of superstars. I never sought out his approval of my abilities. I knew all along I belonged on the short list of great gymnasts. I didn't train hard to please my coaches or make my team's name synonymous with success; I trained hard to squash pity and win for myself.

I have been out of the gymnastics world now for more than twenty years, but I still find ways to prove my physical abilities. Currently, I've taken up an activity I never imagined I would even remotely enjoy: running. I have completed four marathons, numerous half-marathons, and a host of 10K races, with more on the horizon. My greatest achievement thus far is completing the Marine Corps Marathon in 2015 in honor of my grandfather.

My body has been the one constant in my life. Its physical strength allowed me to carry the weight of my world for thirty-three years and, at times, even helped me forget my syndrome. When I was younger, I spent time at water parks, and on numerous occasions the lifeguards questioned whether I was a gymnast. My muscles drew attention away from my face, away from the scars, and away from my hearing aid. In the years when my syndrome was much more pronounced than in the present, I craved that deflection of attention. My physical strength became the diversion I relied on to hold my self-confidence. While my surroundings, friends, and even face have changed over time, my body remains a steady source of personal gratification. By continuing to focus on that physical strength, I forget about the physical flaws caused by my Treacher Collins syndrome.

I continue to nurse the need to prove myself daily. It's that fight, that determination, that drives me. I shouldn't have to do this. I shouldn't have been forced to build a bubble of positivity around myself to banish the crippling opinions of outsiders. No one should face judgmental limitations. Just because I don't look the same as everyone else doesn't mean I'm not smart or creative or athletic.

No one ever told me to my face that I couldn't do something, but at times the implication lingered. Ignorance fueled my determination. I'm thankful for everyone who thought my Treacher Collins syndrome limited me; their doubts only made me stronger. Even if no one ever doubted my abilities and I imagined it all, I flourished thinking they did.

I once believed that God chose the strongest people to struggle because they would be the most likely to rise from the rubble relatively unscathed. As I grew older, and undoubtedly wiser, I realized that not everyone who struggles prospers. Strength couldn't possibly be a derivative of divine intervention when so many people succumb to their adversities. Those who embody great mental strength are not preselected in the womb to be born with such a trait; they make a conscious decision at some point in their lives to adopt that quality and build on it as they grow. A long time ago, I was in a position where I could choose a path of failure or a path of success. I chose to walk the line of success with unwavering courage, fierceness, and strength. And that has made all the difference.

MAY 11, 1988 | *Pat:*

It's time for Kristin's second facial reconstructive surgery. Earlier today I brought her to preschool and explained to her classmates that God made everyone differently. This afternoon she would be admitted to the hospital and her doctor would construct more cheekbones. I explained that she would eventually be joining them in school again but would be very bruised on her face. She'll still be able to have fun with them, but she'll need to be careful. They seemed to understand and are already excited for her return.

We're now at the hospital for registration and admittance. Yesterday Kristin's grandparents surprised us at the house. They drove all the way down from Massachusetts to be here for her surgery. They mean well, but these hospital visits are emotional enough without the added stress of extra family members in the picture. We should be concentrating on the needs of our daughter, not finding ways to entertain her grandparents.

I couldn't tell my in-laws to stay home today. They drove 1,400 miles just to support their granddaughter. And if they were joining us, I had to invite my parents as well. Now I feel as if we are a traveling band of six comical adults sitting in a children's hospital bedroom. The commotion we are making over this blonde-haired five-year-old is astronomical.

Both sets of grandparents marvel at how much Kristin enjoys the attention of the doctors and nurses. She seems unfazed by the revolving door of staff coming in to run tests and prepare for tomorrow. The jovial mood slowly deteriorated when the realization of Kristin's future state hit everyone. Her dad and I had sat helplessly for over seven hours during the previous surgery, and her post-operative condition had gravely saddened us. One of the doctors from that surgery came to pay us a visit, and though he meant well, he recounted traumatic details of the last experience and emphasized how difficult it was to intubate Treacher Collins patients. We really didn't want to focus on any of this the day prior to putting our daughter in the exact same circumstance.

Soon after that doctor left, the anesthesiologist came into the room and reassured us this intubation process would run smoother. This anesthesiologist was brought in during the whole debacle two years ago. He specializes in using the fiber optic scope, which many others do not, and I no longer trust anyone else with my daughter!

* * *

MAY 12, 1988 | *Pat:*
The hospital allowed me to sleep in the room with Kristin last night. Just like last time, the night proved to be nothing but restless. What mother would really be able to rest with an unsuspecting daughter dozing in the hospital bed next to her? The staff came at 7:30 a.m. to take Kristin into the operating room, and I somehow found myself more composed this time around. It was no longer uncharted territory. It couldn't possibly be as traumatic as last time.

Dr. Wolfe emerged from the operating room four hours later with a much livelier disposition this time around. The entire procedure seemed to run smoother than two years ago. Again he grafted cheekbones using the parietal bone from the side of her skull. He also tried to shape her lower eyelids so they didn't droop as much and filed down the bump on her nose for a smoother bone structure.

Kristin is currently in the recovery room until she wakes up and the anesthesia wears off. Then she'll be moved to the intensive care unit for observation.

* * *

MAY 13, 1988 | *Pat:*

Kristin is now back in a regular hospital room. The staff let me sleep there last night for a few hours after an exhausting day. Dr. Wolfe moved her into the ICU in the evening, and she slept there overnight. Kristin's dad drove to Miami yesterday after work. It's incredibly hard for him to come visit and keep his emotions in check. He sees her in her current state and wants so badly to hold her, but he knows he cannot. To lighten the mood, though, Kristin spoke as soon as she heard his voice.

In the ICU, they needed to use one liter of my donated blood because she'd lost so much of her own in surgery. I'm incredibly relieved to have donated this time around. I have decided to donate before each surgery. I'd rather tread cautiously. If they never use the blood, someone else can have it, but I want to ensure my baby has my blood, not some stranger's.

We're learning that each operation may result in different side effects. For example, anesthesia can affect a person differently after each instance. Last time, it seemed to pass through Kristin's system without wreaking havoc. This time, after drinking some apple juice, she immediately spit it up. The remaining anesthesia in her system, combined with excess blood and mucus, caused an unfavorable reaction. The incision below her left eye also began to bleed, causing the nurses to place ice packs on the eye in hopes of accelerating the healing process. Everyone tells me they love having Kristin as a patient; she's so easygoing and doesn't cause the staff any aggravation.

Through all of this, Kristin just wanted to go back into a regular room. We may still be in the hospital, but the regular rooms are less mechanical in nature and more private. In the ICU, all patients are placed in a single open room with the beds separated by curtains. Even though Kristin cannot see or hear the commotion, she can sense it. The regular rooms intimidate her much less.

So here we sit in room 210. All four of the grandparents have come to visit, bringing with them presents from themselves, their friends, and Kristin's preschool classmates. She truly is loved, and I hope one day she understands that.

We started forcing more fluids and some soft food like gelatin into her system. She lies in her bed with a bandaged head and stitched eyes. She becomes more swollen as the day progresses, but that is to be expected. I try to explain to Kristin everything that continues to happen around her: the IV tube in her arm, the constant application of ice packs on her eyes, the need to drink fluids, and the numerous shots. She's so grown up and accepts everything in stride.

* * *

MAY 15, 1988 | *Pat:*
Kristin has been discharged, and we are heading home. The bandage around her head has been removed, but we will visit Dr. Wolfe in his office later this week to remove the stitches. Kristin is thrilled to be in the car putting increasing distance between herself and the hospital. She has already requested spaghetti and meatballs for dinner!

Suddenly this operation has become another blip in her history book. We are so glad to see her returning to her normal self. It reassures us that we made the best decision for our daughter. All of these situations will be in the distant past before we know it. That makes each operation a bit more bearable.

Almost as crucial as teaching me to live an unlimited life, my parents believed in the importance of creating a safe environment for me, one in which I would be surrounded by non-judgmental people, people who would foster self-acceptance instead of self-deprecation. Despite the convenience of having a public elementary school in our backyard, they decided to enroll me in a private Catholic school, where I would receive my kindergarten to eighth-grade education. The public schools in the area were overcrowded, and I faced a greater chance of ridicule from my peers due to the sheer number of students enrolled there. On the other hand, my private elementary school, St. Jude Academy, consisted of only one class per grade, and the school's core, everyday teachings worked to instill morals and values into their students.

No matter what they learn in school, kids can still be cruel. Even my Catholic school class, which consisted of roughly twenty-five students, had problems. Sometimes children resorted to name-calling and bullying. Several students were affected by it. Once my classmates grew out of their childlike innocence and learned words such as "ugly," "fat," and "nerdy," the quiet, lonely kids became the immediate targets of the bullies. For whatever reason, they left me alone and I ventured through my schooling unscathed.

As my childhood friends would later recall, I would be the first to greet the new students in school, making them feel like they had an immediate friend in their time of need. Perhaps my approachable and welcoming personality kept me out of the line of verbal fire. Though I remained relatively quiet and earned high grades, my smiles may have offered me protection.

Another explanation could have been that from the very moment I stepped into the halls of St. Jude Academy, I had an advantage: friends. Some of the students from my preschool class joined me in this grade school. The awkwardness that my appearance may have caused them at one time dissolved into the back of their minds long ago. They were used to my unusual appearance by now. They didn't see me as a girl with a syndrome; they saw me as a normal girl who loved to play and create, just as they did. These kids had also seen me through my last surgery, so nothing came as a shock to them anymore.

Because these old friends showed no adverse reaction to my appearance, I believe the other kindergarteners that had just entered the school became completely blind to my situation as well. These new kids witnessed me playing with my friends and probably figured if those classmates accepted me, they might as well accept me too. All it would have taken was one child to declare me to be a cast-off, and I might have been shunned. But I had already been accepted. And if any peer did try to poke fun at me, I maintained a pretty influential support system of friends who would shut down that nonsense on the spot.

As children grow out of their purity and enter their hormonal stages of adolescence, life becomes a bit more complicated, even in my case. Sixth grade was an uncommonly "off" year. Though it marked the beginning of middle school, I remained in the same private Catholic institution alongside a majority of the same peers. We were all coming into our own at this age. Everyone else seemed to want to mature quickly, but I found contentment in my youth. I had never been in a hurry to grow up, but it was hard not to when the entire class developed pubescent attitudes. Cliques slowly formed, and those who had never uttered an unkind word began to spew them out in an attempt to fit in. I had been on the receiving end of a few of those insults, but not because of my syndrome. My refusal to conform to the middle school agenda made me an easy target. I didn't yet shave my legs, I preferred not to listen to Green Day, and I rarely shopped at PacSun. My priorities revolved around school and gymnastics, not makeup and boys. Once we all came to terms with our new status in life, the teasing slowed. Some friendships faded while others flourished, but by the following year, everyone forgot what had made them crazed.

In seventh grade, a new girl, Elizabeth, joined our class midway through the year. At her old school, she was the victim of incessant teasing spurred by everything from her braces to acne. In preparation for joining her new school, our principal sent her the prior year's yearbook to acquaint her with the soon-to-be-familiar faces. She flipped open the book to find her future classmates and immediately noticed the photo of the first girl listed alphabetically: me. Relief overcame Elizabeth, she told me years later. Surely I, with my facial deformity, would draw any negative attention away from the aspects that caused her tremendous grief at her former middle school.

The day came for Elizabeth to start at St. Jude. She quickly realized that not only did I avoid being bullied, but my peers also admired me. We became fast friends, and over time, the attitude I carried toward my situation changed her perspective on hers. Everything she had previously endured seemed less and less significant. My actions taught her that it shouldn't matter what other people thought of her. In a way, my strength helped her close the door on her past and open the door to healing.

When I quit gymnastics in the middle of eighth grade, my mom pleaded with me to press on for a few more years. I would soon enter high school, and she feared the outcome if I didn't have a reliable source of guidance through this venture into a completely new environment. In gymnastics, I surrounded myself with like-minded, goal-oriented individuals driven by passion and success. The gym and these girls were my second family. They offered another layer of support and acceptance that my mom anticipated I would need as I forged further into my teen years.

Gymnastics was the straight and narrow path, the safe path. But by then I had reached my breaking point and I could no longer find solace in the constant pressure of practices and competitions. I chose to leave the protection of my past and dive headlong into the unknown. I entered my formative high school years without my identity as a gymnast. But again, my parents chose a small Catholic school for the next phase of my growth and education, and this proved to be an exceptionally wise decision.

Many of my former classmates at St. Jude also enrolled at Pope John Paul II High School, and we maneuvered through the halls of uncertainty together. Again, I had friends by my side from the very start, and I surprisingly avoided any conflict during my four years there. Though I have nothing to draw comparisons with, I believe I fared better in a more intimate environment than I would have in an overpopulated mélange of teenage personalities in a public high school. I don't think I could have handled the drama of so many young people teeming with raging hormones. I might not have proof of this, but never would I desire a trip back in time to determine otherwise.

My friends never dwelled on my facial anomaly. After we bonded, they never viewed me as unique. It's as if over time all of my physical flaws blurred into perfect form. Just as I often forgot about my syndrome, they did too.

My friend at Stonehill College, Gina, once confessed to me that the first time she saw me in the cafeteria during the early months of our freshman year, an immediate sense of melancholy washed over her. She said I was filling up my plate at the salad bar unaware that her eyes were following me. She thought she might have gazed a little too long, but she was secretly wondering about everything I had endured during my eighteen years. She felt glum thinking about the number of rude comments I must have received, the constant staring, and all the surgeries I must have suffered through. But as quickly as that sadness filled her, she said she realized I must have built immense internal strength to counteract the negativity in my life. She recognized that I probably worked diligently to earn my spot in this great college, and since I hadn't acknowledged the other students doing double takes when they noticed me, I must have learned to cope with my situation long ago.

When Gina and I met, we became instant friends. She witnessed how my personality outshone my physical abnormality, and any concerns she once harbored about my facial differences disintegrated. Like the many friends before her, she lost sight of my Treacher Collins syndrome and saw me only as Kristin. When she would speak about me to her family, she never once mentioned my condition. And really, if she lost sight of my TCS, why would she even bring it up to them? When she eventually introduced us, her family instantly loved my jovial personality. Afterward, of course, they had plenty of questions for Gina about my situation, and it was only then that she realized it had never occurred to her to mention my syndrome prior to our meeting. In her eyes, there was nothing unusual about me. Over the years, her family grew to become my family, and now I am solely Kristin to them as well.

The closer my friendships grew, the more those friends wanted to fight my battles for me. They became increasingly more cognizant of the daily struggles I faced the more time they spent with me in public. I'm aware that even adults stare, just as Gina pointed out. Curiosity never fades. Adults, however, are more inconspicuous than children, so much so that I rarely noticed the inquisitive glances from the adults. Children, though, I couldn't escape no matter how hard I tried.

My childhood best friend, Meghan, and I grew close after our teacher forced us to merge our separate gymnastics routines into one for the first-grade talent show. Prior to then, we hadn't spent much time together out of the confines of our school. That talent show performance allowed us to bond over our commonalities and realize that a potential friendship stared us right in our faces. From that point forward, we were inseparable.

Meghan and I spent many weekends venturing to the attractions in Central Florida with our families. We coordinated our outfits well in advance and begged our parents to tell anyone who asked that we were sisters. It frustrated Meghan to witness the constant gawking over my facial deformity when she no longer noticed my flaws herself. One day, my normally soft-spoken friend couldn't control her anger. We were in line for a roller-coaster ride when she noticed a group of young teenagers whispering to each other with their eyes fixated on me. As we rounded the corner in line and passed them, she bluntly asked, "Why are you staring at my sister?" Shocked that someone, let alone a nine-year-old, noticed what they were doing and called them out on their rude actions, they responded with utter silence. Meghan's question may not have yielded an answer, but it halted the whispers. Silence is a precious gift to me, especially when it can stop my pain.

My face continued to attract attention despite the number of surgeries I endured. As I aged, I gained even more friends who began to experience the same frustrations as Meghan. Gina and I traveled to Orlando, Florida, for spring break during our sophomore year of college. While walking around the theme parks, she took note of every child who inquisitively gazed or commented on my looks. This infuriated her. She had never experienced this unwanted attention in such force since we mainly stayed on the college campus, a somewhat controlled environment. Here, she ached for me. As their eyes bore into my features, she wanted nothing more than to scold them and knock some sense into their parents for allowing their rude behavior to occur. Gina experienced the same emotional roller-coaster I rode every time I appeared in public from the moment I was born. The unsettled knot formed in her stomach, just as it always had in mine.

Friends weren't the only key partners in my life who tried to divert any negative attention. My grandparents would continually share my gymnastics success with strangers. Their gloating seemed like unnecessary outbursts at the time, but I now understand the weight of their intent. "She's a state-champion gymnast," my grandma would tell anyone in earshot. "She earned a perfect ten on the floor exercise." These verbal acknowledgments helped my grandparents cope with the wandering eyes they saw stay focused on my face for a moment too long. We'd be standing patiently in line for a ride, and my grandma would make some unprovoked comment to the person ahead of her. This always embarrassed me. I accepted the attention I earned while performing in my competitions, but in my everyday life, I would have preferred to remain unnoticed. Not that I welcomed gawking, but I wished my grandparents had let onlookers stare without feeling the need to prove to them my worth. In truth, they weren't preaching my accomplishments solely for my benefit. While these validating statements were the only way they knew how to protect me, speaking such truths also helped them heal their breaking hearts.

Family played a major role in creating a nontoxic environment, just as much as my friendships and schooling. Aside from my parents, who obviously made me feel completely secure and loved, my extended relatives also treated me just as any ordinary child. Every summer I would spend a week or two in Massachusetts visiting my family and soaking in the northern way of life. Though my two cousins, Marina and Melina, were seven and eight years younger than I, I latched on to the love they shared from the get-go. As young children, they never once questioned my appearance, which I found uncommon. In my experience, the younger in age, the more blatantly curious children are. Their presence comforted me, because though they were innocent, they were wise beyond their years. When told I would be having another surgery, they would respond with, "But why, Mommy? She is beautiful. I want to look just like her." No one ever said that about me. *I* never said that about me.

Never once did they press me about my syndrome, not even when they grew to be more intelligent and observant. We saw each other infrequently, so one would assume at some point their young minds would forget me and need to re-assimilate to my unique appearance the following summer. But that never happened. They always greeted me by jumping off the couch and gathering me into a bear hug when I walked through the front door of their house. The only look I ever received from them was love, and that is perhaps why I consider them to be more like my sisters than my cousins. They found me perfectly imperfect and loved me unconditionally.

All of these relationships saved me, friendships and family alike, while my environment protected me. It caused me to forget that the reality I lived in included abnormal doctor's visits and constant scrutiny. It built me up rather than slowly unravel me. It encouraged me to move through life without trepidation.

As a child, I interacted with others wherever I went. I lived a carefree and unassuming life. If I saw children playing on the swing set, I would join in on the excitement without hesitation. The world was my playground, and I found no excuse great enough—not even my syndrome—to prevent me from experiencing the thrills.

My parents encouraged me to make friends. They grasped that it might not always turn out favorably, but they never prevented an opportunity for me to assimilate with other children. While at a University of Miami football game, I began interacting with a few other kids in the surrounding rows of seats. We played within view of our parents but out of earshot of them. Eventually, an older boy came over to tell my dad that his friend was "messing" with me. Not exactly sure what was happening, my dad scooped me up and we returned to our seats to finish watching the game. I was only about three years old, too young to understand the sensitivity around my situation, and didn't realize that I had been the butt of some kid's jokes. Even as a toddler, if you put yourself out there, you risk rejection.

As I aged, I grew more self-aware and hesitated to interact with new people. Talking became a chore rather than a part in an imaginative situation. It meant exposing parts of myself, whether I wanted to or not. Childhood involved playing more so than talking. Playing was effortless. Conversing required skill, energy, and a willingness to listen. These days, I'm cautious with my relationships. I appear more standoffish, but in actuality, I'm observing. I want to continue to surround myself with people who inspire me and share the same values, so I take my time before allowing outsiders into my life.

My parents did the most they could to ensure my quality of life remained high. Of course, they couldn't shelter me from all negative fallout. Not all parents teach their children to be accepting and welcoming. That's just an unfortunate reality. There will always be a girl on the playground who refuses to play with children like me because the unknown frightens her. I hope that children like me have a support system they can depend on to lift them up when they're down. My parents, family, and friends knew exactly how to love and accept my imperfections, allowing me to thrive in a nurturing environment.

JUNE 13, 1990 | *Chris:*

Another summer, another surgery. The poor kid can't catch a break. This whole process feels especially routine now, with one difference this time: Kristin seems to comprehend the struggles that lie in the days ahead. Last night she asked to sleep over at a friend's house. Her mom and I questioned if she would be able to handle it with the operation looming in the near future, but we let her go anyway. Maybe she felt no anxiety whatsoever; maybe she just needed an outlet to help her forget.

As night fell and we didn't hear from her, we felt she must have been enjoying the free time before captivity. No sooner than we turned out the lights, the phone rang. A tiny, wavering voice on the other end wanted to come home for the night. That confirmed to us that she absolutely understood the weight of the next few days and severe measures it entailed.

We drove down to the children's hospital this afternoon. Upon arrival, the nursing staff sent Kristin for a chest x-ray. As her mom and I watched her lie there on the machine, an unfamiliar feeling washed over me. I became angry with Kristin. I became angry because she made all of us, including herself, go through this entire process again. Three previous surgeries and who knows how many more in the future, all caused by a mutated gene.

Fear and frustration do that to even the best people. They lay blame where it doesn't belong. I felt fearful for my daughter, and that fear turned into anger toward her. I was actually enraged at the situation, not at my daughter. I detested every single needle that pricked her innocent skin. I despised not being able to change fate with a snap of my fingers.

As I continued to stand on the side helplessly watching, I shook my head free from the invading thoughts of misplaced anger. This was in no way Kristin's fault. It wasn't any of our faults. And just like that I replaced resentment with worry, the only emotion I should have felt from the start. I'll never forgive myself for those infuriating thoughts, but I am human.

We're gathered in Kristin's hospital room now getting her ready for bed. Our normally lively girl stares blankly at the cartoons on television. Her silence is a telltale sign of the fear coursing through her veins. Only in times of uneasiness does she remain still and quiet. She remembers the pain, trauma, and needles, which causes her demeanor to make this shift. Fear radiates from her eyes as she knows well what lies ahead: more incisions, stitches, and scars. Those are benign compared to the constant prodding and poking when she can't see or hear the surrounding environment. Without the sense of sight and sound, Kristin can't assess situations, and that unknown ignites the greatest amount of fear.

Pretty soon I'll head home for the night, bringing the dread of tomorrow with me. One would think we would be used to this by now. I'm not certain that day will ever arrive.

* * *

JUNE 14, 1990 | *Chris:*

As I sit here at work waiting for an update from Kristin's mother, I can't help but hope that one day Kristin will understand how much I love her and how helpless this all makes me feel. A father can only do so much, but "so much" isn't nearly enough. While she endures the physical pain, I share the emotional. If I cannot take her place on the surgical table, I should be able to appear strong for her.

* * *

JUNE 15, 1990 | *Pat:*

After the nurses wheeled Kristin into the operating room yesterday morning, I laced up my running shoes for a jaunt through the Coral Gables neighborhoods. This has become my routine. Once I know Kristin has successfully been placed under anesthesia, I release all of my frustrations out on the pavement. I find it helps my mind focus and enables me to better care for my daughter once she transfers to the intensive care unit. I discover a solace on those roads that I could never feel sitting in a stiff waiting room chair.

The operation went smoothly. The same anesthesiologist administered the intubation with ease. Dr. Wolfe performed the same craniotomy as last time. Kristin lies in her hospital room bandaged, stitched, and swollen, but everything seems a bit easier this time. We have familiarized ourselves with the recovery process and foresee a smooth road of healing.

* * *

JUNE 18, 1990 | *Pat:*

Dr. Wolfe scheduled Kristin's discharge for tomorrow! This hospital stay has been much easier than the rest. Trying, of course, but somehow less intrusive. Kristin is thrilled to continue her recovery on the living room couch as soon as possible.

A nice young couple from Key West admitted their baby this afternoon and now shares the double room with us. As we find ourselves completing a round of procedures, this couple reminds us that someone else's journey starts as ours ends. The hospital rooms entertain a revolving door of patients, each with their own unique tale. As we prepare to wave goodbye to the stresses of the last few days, this couple now dons the essential brave faces worn by the parents of each patient.

To celebrate our family's elation and ease the new couple's minds, we snuck pizza and wine into the hospital room. Kristin continued to watch television as us parents bonded over the trials and tribulations of feeling helpless over our children. This last night couldn't have been more perfect. For once, we celebrated a night in the hospital instead of dreading it. I'm not sure when we'll return here, though I pray not for quite a while, but I now see hope for the future.

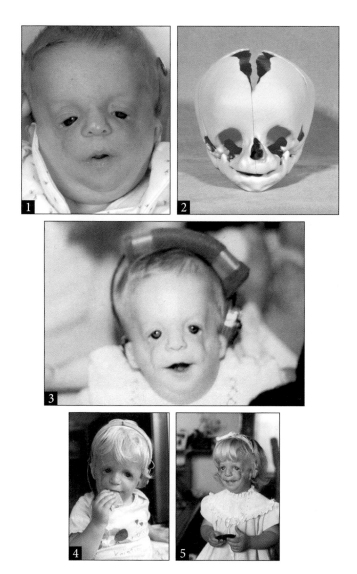

1. Two months old, my first photo taken at Dr. Wolfe's office.
2. Representation of a Treacher Collins skull. 3. Four months old.
4. Ten months old. 5. Two years old.

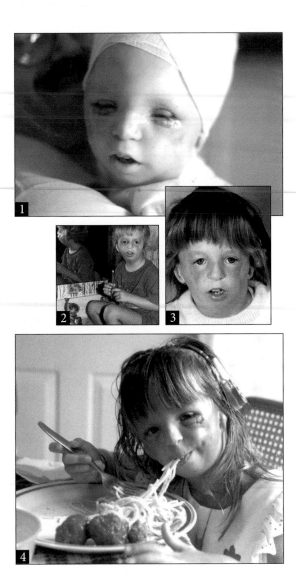

1. Three years old, after my first major surgery in 1986.
2. Five years old, putting on makeup and realizing for the first time that my features are different from my mother's. 3. Five years old, pre-surgery in 1988.
4. Five years old, the day I was released from the hospital.
I asked for spaghetti and meatballs for dinner.

1. My sixth birthday. 2. Seven years old, with my parents, Chris and Pat.
3. Eight years old with my first gymnastics medal.
4. Nine years old, receiving a perfect-10 gymnastics score.
5. Eleven years old, posing for my yearly American Twisters Gymnastics photo. 6. Thirteen years old, showing off my physique.

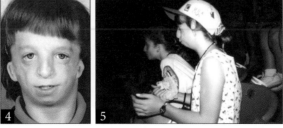

1. Ten years old with cousins Melina (left) and Marina (right).
2. Eleven years old. 3. Ten years old with my friend Meghan.
4. Twelve years old. 5. Thirteen years old. My chin has
not yet been developed.

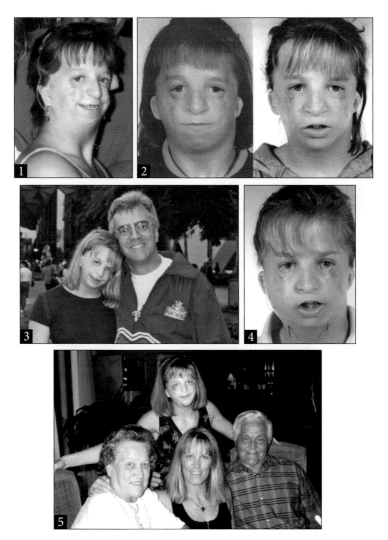

1. Fourteen years old, one month from major surgery. 2. Fourteen years old, before and after surgery. 3. Fifteen years old, with Dad. 4. Sixteen years old, with my jaw distraction device in place. 5. Sixteen years old after the device was removed, with my grandparents and my mom.

1. Seventeen years old. 2. Twenty years old,
after major surgery in 2003. 3. Nineteen years old.
4. Twenty-one years old, with college friend Gina.

1. Twenty-two years old, before surgery in 2005. 2. With best friend Lisa after the '05 surgery. 3. Twenty-three years old, with Meghan, after the cornea transplant in 2006. 4. Twenty-four years old, after surgery in 2007. 5. Twenty-six years old, in Athens, Greece.

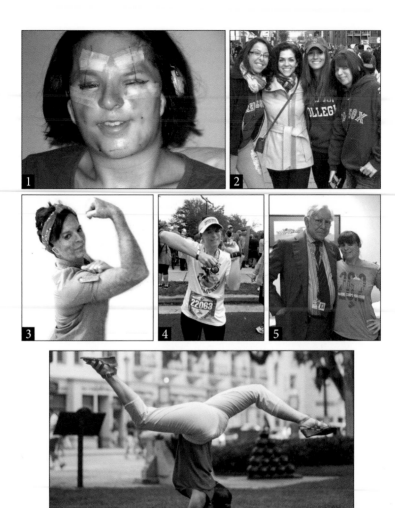

1. Twenty-seven years old, after my last surgery, in 2010.
2. Thirty years old with Lisa (left), Marina, and Melina. 3. Thirty-one years old. I can do it! 4. Thirty-two years old, after the Marine Corps Marathon.
5. Thirty-three years old, with Dr. Wolfe in 2016.
6. Thirty-three years old. Once a gymnast, always a gymnast.

My syndrome ruled my life whether I wanted it to or not. One fact I couldn't ignore was that my facial features were much smaller than other people's my age. But it wasn't just the visual impact of my small features that affected me; it also had to do with the functionality of some of those features. Sure, everyone noticed my tiny ears, but no one really took notice of the size of my mouth, which I couldn't even open wide enough to suck on a Blow Pop.

As my baby teeth began to fall out, it became evident that my mouth couldn't comfortably hold all of my permanent teeth. Severe crowding would occur if nothing was done. At the age of ten, I began routine visits to an oral surgeon to extract a total of fourteen teeth. The surgeon determined which teeth would be unnecessary and devised a plan to remove a few at a time. This included baby teeth, as well as the permanent teeth that had not yet broken through. The baby teeth were easy to remove, but the permanent teeth required that the surgeon painstakingly dig below the surface until all remnants were gone.

The oral surgeon performed these procedures over about four different appointments, including one to remove two of the four wisdom teeth sitting below the surface of my gums. During each visit, I was a ball of nerves as I sat in the waiting room. If an appointment ran late, I would attempt to fall asleep in the waiting room chair, hoping the surgeon would simply start the procedure while I dozed. Of course, that never happened and my dad would wake me when the nurse called my name. A couple of times, I worked my nerves into such a frenzy that I knocked myself out cold. My dad tried for almost a minute to rouse me from my anxiety-ridden slumber; finally I woke up realizing the nightmare had not yet begun.

I dreaded those appointments. As I reclined in the chair, the surgeon administered the Novocain and would forcibly open my mouth wider than I thought possible until all teeth were removed; then I had to listen to the squealing of the drill as it burrowed beneath my gums. I remember the constant pressure from the surgeon trying the yank the tooth free from the grips of its comfortable place in my mouth and wondering when it would end. After the teeth were yanked and the stitches sewn in place, I would leave the office biting down on lumps of gauze until the bleeding subsided. My gums and cheeks would stay numb for hours after the procedures, and when I tried to eat meals of soft spaghetti with butter and cheese, the noodles would cling to my face without my knowledge.

Just like everything else, the extraction procedures eventually ended; I was free to resume my normal life, but my sense of normalcy now included a new source of trauma ingrained into my memory.

I still face anxiety over even routine visits to the dentist, because I fear they will tell me more work needs to be done, a tooth needs to be pulled, or a cavity has formed. Depending on the positioning of my head and the extent to which my mouth is forced open, I cannot breathe during an oral procedure, and this frightens me. Only one of my two remaining wisdom teeth has ever formed. I fear the day that it needs to be removed, because I'm certain it would require breaking my jaw in order to perform the extraction. I hope I never receive that news from the dentist. Then again, before each visit, I always prepare myself for the worst.

Sometimes I wonder if the pain of having my wisdom tooth removed would be better than constantly feeling anxious about the possibility of it being removed. Living with such anxiety makes for a very frightening life, and at this point, I'm not really certain I can live with that fear forever. It might be time to do what I've been dreading for so long.

The tiny size of my mouth and the multiple necessary extractions directly tied back to my Treacher Collins syndrome; however, in sixth grade, the universe pitched me an unexpected curveball, which in no way related to my facial anomaly. While out to dinner with my family, I mentioned the vision in my right eye seemed a bit blurry. My dad decided to test my vision as we looked over the menu. He held the menu up to my eye level, slowly moved it toward me, and told me to say "stop" at the distance I could read it. I tried my hardest to refuse this game, but I eventually surrendered and covered my right eye. The knot in my stomach tangled into a giant mess with each breath. I knew this game couldn't possibly end well. "Stop," I grudgingly replied when my eye focused on the lettering.

I then covered my left eye and repeated the process. Slowly the menu crept toward my face and I tried to sort through the blur of colors I saw. Closer. Closer. Closer. I could sense the concern this caused my parents and grandparents. Closer. Closer. "Stop." The menu paused a half an inch away from my face.

The last time I had my eyes tested at school, I passed the vision test with ease. When was that exactly? Kindergarten? First grade? I don't know. Nor do I have the slightest idea when my vision took a turn for the worse, but by this age, I really only used my left eye to focus on the details surrounding me. In gymnastics, I completed my skills on the balance beam by focusing on the object in the middle; I generally saw three balance beams because of my poor eyesight, and it seemed logical to me that the real beam was the middle one. I was usually right.

I never let on that I struggled to see, but I don't suppose I ever really identified my poor eyesight as a problem to myself. I had dealt with other, more important issues my entire life, and this complication was just another irritation to add to my existing list of troubles. My eyesight didn't need to be corrected right away, though, so I simply learned to maneuver around my less-than-stellar vision while keeping it a secret.

The mood at dinner that night tensed after the makeshift vision test. By the time we returned home after the meal, my dad handed me a large travel book and repeated the menu test with the gigantic lettering on the cover of this book. Different prop, same result. Something was obviously wrong.

The following morning, my dad phoned a local eye doctor and snatched the first possible appointment. He planned to get to the bottom of this as soon as possible. I could tell this recent development frightened my family, but I took it in stride. Little did I know I was on my way down another uncharted path requiring constant follow-up. I didn't face the typical blurred vision scenario that could be swiftly corrected by a pair of spectacles. No simple nearsightedness or farsightedness here. No. We learned another word that day: keratoconus.

Apparently, my senses enjoyed playing games on me. Not only did I have a condition affecting my hearing, I now also had a second condition, this one affecting my vision. In keratoconus, the cornea forms abnormally. Rather than developing into the usual rounded formation, the cornea bulges out into the shape of a cone. That day,

I learned that this irregular shape distorted my vision and could worsen over time. It would require me to visit two more specialists: an ophthalmologist who concentrated on corneal diseases and a contact lens specialist for rigid, gas-permeable lenses.

The keratoconus had developed in both of my eyes, but not at the same rate. I still saw pretty clearly out of my left eye, even without a contact lens; however, the poor vision in my right eye constituted legal blindness. I could distinguish between various shapes of objects when an illustration was presented to me, but I could identify no other details about those objects. When reading the eye chart, I could only tell where the top of the chart was, and also identify the largest letter, E, but everything else appeared fuzzy.

My ophthalmologist conducted a special test using a corneal topography machine to discern the exact severity of the condition in both eyes. This machine mapped out the surface curvature of the cornea much like the topography of a landscape. Each color matched a level of sloping. The warmer the color, the steeper the slope. I gazed into the viewfinder with my left eye and waited anxiously for something to happen. Lights appeared in ring formations, and it almost felt like my eye peered into the depths of a tunnel. The doctor told me to focus on the red dot at the end of the rings of lights.

After a few clicks of the button, I switched sides. With my right eye fixed on the focal point, I now saw three blurred red spots instead of one solid red dot. When my results were printed out, the doctor examined the color charts. My left eye consisted of mostly cool colors, meaning the slope of my cornea had not formed into a steep peak yet. It was manageable. My right eye, however, painted a more colorful picture using all hues of the rainbow. The warmer colors stood out the most and meant my cornea reached a sharp cone. This severe coning caused the distortions and blurred vision.

The most immediate method to improve my vision was with the use of rigid, gas-permeable contact lenses. The lenses are designed to flatten out sloped corneas in order to provide less distortion of light. The only way to improve my keratoconus condition was to try reshaping my cornea. Neither glasses nor soft contacts could force the cornea to hold a specific shape, but hard contacts had that capability. If I didn't take proper measures right away, my keratoconus probably would worsen over time. As for the contact lens, glass can only bend to a certain curvature point before it breaks. Eventually, my coning could become too steep, and no contact lens would be able to fit. I would then need a cornea transplant to correct my vision. The goal was to prevent that from happening until I grew older. If I acted immediately, I lessened the chance of my coning becoming untreatable.

Not all, or even many, ophthalmologists can fit patients for gas-permeable lenses the way they can fit patients for glasses or soft contacts. Hard lenses require more than a simple prescription. Just as runners need to be properly fitted for running sneakers by professionals who can analyze gait and pressure points, contact lens specialists evaluate the curvature of the eye and fit lenses according to the shape of the cornea. This task falls on a select few, especially when dealing with problems such as keratoconus.

My next stop on the road to a cure for keratoconus was Bascom Palmer Eye Institute in Miami, Florida, where I was scheduled to visit a renowned specialist in contact lens fitting. I sat in the waiting room petrified of the road ahead. Would I have this uncomfortable, foreign glass object inserted into my eye? Even if it worked, would I constantly worry about my coning steepening, which would eventually necessitate a cornea transplant? How many times a year would I need to visit these doctors? Would my routine be disrupted? Why was this happening?

Amidst all of these thoughts racing through my mind, the nurse called my name and forced me back into the present. We followed her silently down the hall and into an examination room to wait for the specialist, an optometrist, to join us. Once he did, he walked us through the procedure for fitting these lenses. He squeezed a few drops of medication into my eyes, one being a numbing agent that would prevent my eyes from sensing they had glass lenses in them. He then tried variously shaped contact lenses on each eye until he found the most secure fit for my coning. Once the corneas were reshaped with the gas-permeable lenses, the specialist asked me to look through the phoropter, a prescription testing device. He led me through a series of questions. "What looks better? One or two?" We did this multiple times on both eyes until I had the perfect prescriptions. He popped out the sample contact lenses I currently wore using a miniature plunger and said he would call us as soon as my new lenses were ready. I left empty-handed that day and anxious for the future.

When my gas-permeable lenses arrived at Bascom Palmer several days later, we drove back down to Miami to learn how to assimilate to this new way of life. The specialist numbed my eyes again and placed the lenses on my corneas to ensure we chose the most accurate prescriptions. Then it was time to learn how to insert and remove my new contacts, or "eyes," as I began to refer to them. The specialist walked me through the process step by step.

"You have two different lenses. Because your two corneas cone to a different steepness, your lenses are not interchangeable. Left must always be placed in the left eye, and right in the right eye. First, you wash your hands. Always wash your hands. Then, take the lens for the left eye and place it on your left index finger. Squeeze a drop of solution on it so it's nice and moist. When you're ready, use your fingers on your right hand to hold up the upper eyelid on your left eye. Next, use the middle finger on your left hand to pull down your lower lid. Once your eye is open wide enough, move your left index finger closer to your eye until you feel the lens on top of it. Blink a few times and it will settle in there nicely. Then do the same with the right eye."

Once he placed both lenses on my eyes, he walked me through taking them off using the plunger. "Add a drop of solution onto the plunger and apply it directly onto the lens. It should come right off, but if it doesn't, just try it again. Make sure you put the lenses back into their appropriate cases. Whenever you take these lenses off, you need to wash them. Place the contacts in one of your palms, add a few drops of cleaning solution, and massage the solution into the contacts for thirty to sixty seconds. Rinse off, and then put the lenses back into their cases. Be sure to add enough solution to cover the lenses and keep them wet until your next use. You don't want to dry them out."

All of these instructions overwhelmed me. I'd never had to deal with such a regimen before. My surgeries never required me to follow a set of rules to heal. I usually just had to lie on the couch and do nothing. After hearing these instructions, I thought, what if I messed up? What if I forgot to do something? What if somehow I scratched my corneas? Heat worked its way up my body until beads of sweat formed on every available inch of my skin.

The optometrist instructed me to try this routine myself with him there. He wanted to see how I would do. Reluctantly, I obliged.

I popped the lenses on without much trouble since the numbing agent hadn't yet worn off. I did, however, struggle to remove the lenses. The plunger wouldn't grab hold of the contact. What if it stayed in my eye? What if I had to sleep with it in my eye because I couldn't get it to come off? The sweat oozed out of me now. Oh God, what if it rolled behind my eye? This petrified me, but I wanted the lens off my eye, so I kept at it until I finally managed to find traction.

I left the eye institute terrified of the road ahead. I would start wearing these lenses slowly until my eyes adjusted to the foreign objects, but I already dreaded the following morning when I had to relive this process, only this time without guidance from a trained professional.

The following morning, I woke a little earlier to adapt to my new routine. I arranged my contact lens paraphernalia on the counter of my parents' bathroom sink. I took a breath and began the process. Wash hands, place contact on finger, add drop of solution, hold lids open, here we go … and place the contact onto the eye. *Oh damn! It fell out!* Start process over. *Why won't this go in? OK, it's finally in. Good Lord, this feels strange. Ugh! I wish I had those numbing drops. Why is everything so bright? Oh my God, I have to do this every morning and wear these all day long? How will I survive this torture?*

I did survive. I found some days easier than others. Some mornings, my eyes were too tired to wear my contacts so I left them off that day at school and wore them only for gymnastics. Most weekdays, though, I wore my contacts for fourteen hours a day, from school through the end of gymnastics training. My eyes would dry out, but I did what needed to be done.

My sensitivity to light increased threefold because of my blue eyes, my keratoconus, and, now, my glass contact lenses. Some days the world seemed too bright to function. I would stare at the white page of my textbook, and the reflection of the fluorescent overhead light would blind me. Those days, I tried to focus my attention elsewhere until my eyes calmed down.

I had to admit that having reliable vision in both my eyes helped tremendously. Not only could I see the balance beam again, but also I could see ahead of me. On weekends, I allowed my eyes to rest, and I functioned sans contacts. There were plenty of times my mom and I would be out shopping and I would be oblivious to the people around me. "Kristin, that girl over there just said hi," my mom would say. Not only did I not hear the person, I didn't see her either. When I wore my contacts, however, I noticed everyone.

As the weeks, months, and years passed, I became accustomed to my gas-permeable contacts. I visited my ophthalmologist and cornea specialist as often as necessary. They watched the progression in my slopes and fitted me for new lenses as needed. Because my right cornea had a more pronounced slope, the lens didn't always stay securely in place, even though we consistently ensured I had the proper prescription. It became commonplace for my contact to pop off in the middle of gymnastics practice. As I flipped through the air on the floor exercise, it would detach itself and land on a mat somewhere. I always found it one way or another, once even stuck to the bottom of another gymnast's foot. When I found it, I'd run to the bathroom, clean it, and pop the lens back in. Even though wearing these lenses wasn't always comfortable, it became a much easier process than when I tried to insert them on my own the very first time.

Eventually, my keratoconus felt like just another quirk in my life. It would require constant management throughout my entire life, but it no longer drained me emotionally. Today, I no longer wear my contacts. I've undergone a cornea transplant in my right eye and gave up using a contact in the left. That cornea sloping worsened over the years, making contact wearing difficult. Someday, I'm sure I'll require a transplant in the left eye, but until then, I'm thankful I can see out of one eye unassisted.

JULY 7, 1997 | *Kristin*:

Last October, Dr. Wolfe broke the news that it was finally time for my next surgery. While my parents and I waited for his scheduling manager to determine the best available summer date for the operation, I broke down and wept in the waiting room of his office. I thought my fortune had finally changed. For seven years, I had avoided operations. For seven years, I felt like a normal girl. For seven years, I spent my summers concentrating on my friendships, gymnastics, and enjoying my life rather than recovering from procedures. That seven-year interim made me think that my years of reconstructive surgeries were over. What wishful thinking.

Now it seems my life is reverting back to the way it was in my younger years; my surgeries will begin again in full force. Dr. Wolfe was waiting for my facial bones to further develop before continuing with the reconstruction process. Since that has happened, it's time to focus on more than just my underdeveloped cheekbones. Over the years, my bite worsened as my facial bones grew, and there is now a huge gap between my teeth when I bite down. This surgery will correct that. The plan is to shift my entire jaw, mandible and maxilla, forward. This not only will create a better bite, but also open up my constricted airway. This process involves breaking many facial bones and aligning them into new positions. I am facing an extremely invasive procedure, which will keep me out of commission for a while.

To keep my mind off the difficult surgery ahead, I spent the last two weeks in Massachusetts with my cousins. Being with them and being in a place far from Miami helped me forget about the traumatic path I am about to head down; however, as soon as I arrived back at the Fort Lauderdale airport, my attention immediately turned toward my scheduled operation. It is still a few days away, but I need to visit the orthodontist teaming up with my reconstructive surgeon on this mission. He requires x-rays and molds of my mouth to evaluate the process of my procedure. We're in the car heading to his office now.

My stomach is churning at the thought. I visited this particular orthodontist as a baby, and from all the stories I've heard, he has a rough and nasty temperament. I don't want to leave the care of my current benign orthodontist for someone who acts like a beast, but Dr. Wolfe insists that my orthodontic care be moved to someone who understands the nuances of my scheduled ortho-maxillary surgery. While my current orthodontist knows enough about braces, he does not specialize in the more sensitive matters pertaining to my syndrome. I will be enduring extensive work to the jaw that needs specific monitoring, which only a trained specialist can provide. All of the tension I released in Massachusetts slams back into my body ten times worse. The day of surgery hasn't even arrived but already this is turning into my worst summer yet.

* * *

JULY 9, 1997

The hospital no longer requires us to arrive for preregistration the night before an operation. I fell asleep in my own bed last night thinking that today's reality seemed surreal. But it's not pretend; it's not a fantasy. My surgery day has arrived, and I'm terrified. I'm afraid of all the little things I remember from seven years prior: the needles, the pain, the inability to see and hear. But I'm also petrified of the unknown. This procedure will be more intense than anything I experienced in the past, and I don't quite know what to expect. I don't know what condition I'll be in after the operation or how long I'll be kept in the hospital to recuperate. I just want to go home, lie in my bed, and hide under my covers until the day is over. I don't want to do this, I don't want to be here in the hospital, but I know I don't have a choice. This is my life with Treacher Collins syndrome. This is my normal.

Given my age, fourteen, my operation is scheduled for some time in the afternoon with three other procedures occurring before mine. We arrive at the hospital to register at 11 a.m., but much like my very first experience at Miami Children's Hospital, my surgery is already delayed. The operations prior to mine are lasting longer than planned, and my parents and I sit impatiently in the waiting room as the minutes continue to tick by. At some point, my dad and I decide to pace the sterile halls of the hospital for an hour or two, trying not to focus on the fateful hours to come. Unlike my cleft palate surgery when I was only eighteen months old, I'm fully aware of what awaits me. The nerves, fear, and anticipation have left me feeling like a ticking time bomb. If the staff doesn't take me back to the pre-op area soon, I'm going to run out of the hospital and not return.

As the late afternoon rolls around, the nurses finally walk us back to the pre-operation area, an open room with individual stations divided by curtains for privacy. I sit anxiously on the chair next to my dad, waiting for the nurses to come back. So much time has lapsed since I sat in this very room, yet it feels both familiar and foreign at the same time. I know enough to be terrified, but I don't know of what.

The nurse joins us to take a vial of blood for my chart. I can handle a finger prick like they do at my pediatrician's office, but the hospital requires more blood than what comes from a finger prick. I have been traumatized over the years with nurses having difficulty finding the veins in my arms, so I squeeze my dad's hand as hard as I can to take my mind off of the needle. Luckily, this nurse doesn't have any trouble and as soon as she removes the needle from my arm, I release the breath I'd been holding.

My fear hasn't completely dissipated yet. I know there's a shot of medication coming, and my mind continues to think about needles puncturing my body. As it turns out, some things have changed over the last seven years and the hospital no longer administers the calming medication through a shot. Instead, the nurse hands me a small plastic cup filled with purple liquid, the new calming medicine. It tastes absolutely horrible, but I can handle it, especially if it means no shot.

After I slip into my hospital gown and snuggle up under the blankets of my hospital bed, I wait to be wheeled into the operating room. Dr. Wolfe and my anesthesiologist come to say a quick hello, and then it is time. I drift deeper into a hazy fog as a nurse wheels my bed away from my parents and into the surgical room. Theodore, my trusted teddy bear, stays at my side.

Someone places a mask over my face and tells me to breathe. Looking around, everything has a dizzying effect from the medication so I decide to close my eyes instead. One of the nurses grabs my right hand and tells me I will feel a couple of pinches. "Squeeze my hand and say, 'Ouch, ouch, ouch'," she instructs. When I feel the needle near my ankle, I do just that. And then again in my wrist. The IV tubes are now in place, and it is time for me to drift off to sleep.

"Count backward from ten, Kristin," someone directs me.

"Ten, nine, eight, sev..."

* * *

JULY 10-11, 1997

I don't know when I woke up after the surgery, but I'm told the entire procedure lasted until about seven at night. My eyes are swollen shut so I can't see the time. My head is bandaged so I can't wear my hearing aid. I have no idea what is going on around me. How long have I been lying here? What day is it? I drift in and out of consciousness as life in the intensive care unit continues around me.

In the moments I'm awake, I think I hear beeping, constant beeping, and the dial tone I hear when I connect to AOL. Is this all in my head? Why would someone be connecting to AOL here? And why does my hip hurt so much? I had surgery on my face, and I surprisingly only notice the pressure from the swelling, but no real pain as I would have thought with broken bones.

I hear the nurse ask me a question from somewhere far in the distance. "Kristin, are you in pain? Do you want some morphine?"

I manage a barely audible, "No."

"She doesn't like needles." I hear my mom tell the nurse. "Kristin, you have an IV hooked up. You won't need a shot. The morphine will come through the IV. Are you in pain? Do you want some?"

"Yes, my hip hurts," I slur. The nurse fulfills my wish as my mom explains that Dr. Wolfe had taken hipbone to use in my cheeks instead of the usual parietal bone. He was running out of bone to use from my skull without creating a potentially dangerous scenario.

I drift off to sleep again and dream I am a beeper, like the one my doctor wears, swimming in the depths of the ocean. Suddenly, I can't breathe. I'm drowning. It feels so real. Why does it feel so real? I force myself awake and somehow begin to breathe again.

At some point—minutes, hours, days later, I can't tell—Dr. Wolfe comes to check on my progression. This was a very tedious procedure, and the swelling impacted my ability to breathe properly. Because of this, he kept me on a respirator to control my breathing when I first emerged from the operating room; however, he notices that the breathing tube is still snaking its way through my nose and he's angry. He never intended the tube to be in place for this long. He wants it gone immediately and rips it out of my body. I feel the world close in on me as the tube travels up my throat and out of my nose. I can't breathe! I arch my spine and throw my head back trying somehow to open up my airway. There's not much I can do, but choke, cough, and gasp for breath until I finally inhale enough air to calm myself down. I feel helpless because my lack of sight and hearing leaves me completely unaware of my surroundings.

Even though I never know what's about to happen, I have my mom to be my eyes and ears. She stays by my side the entire time I'm lying in the ICU. She only leaves when she has to, but immediately rejoins me as soon as the nursing staff allows her back in. I know she returns when she grabs my hand and begins to squeeze it. This is our signal. I feel more comfortable knowing she's next to me, and the nurses don't mind, either, since my mom acts as my own personal aide. By now, she knows the drill. She keeps a watchful eye on my situation, which allows the ICU staff to focus on the other patients. When I beg for more morphine, she mentions it to the nurses. If I need to be cleaned, she helps. And when I need soothing, she squeezes my hand.

JULY 12, 1997

Dr. Wolfe keeps me in the intensive care unit for only three days, but to me it seems like a lifetime. As soon as I am well enough, the staff transports me to a shared hospital room. The swelling around my eyes has subsided just enough that I can tell I have the half of the room next to the wall-to-wall window. My vision is still impaired from swelling, but the sunlight adds welcomed warmth to the room. I can feel it.

Dr. Wolfe removes the bandage from my head, and I am able to finally wear my hearing aid again. I can't see the television too well, but I can hear it. And when I'm tired of listening to the Disney Channel (it's a children's hospital, after all), I listen to music on my portable CD player. I'm not as comfortable as I would be at home, but this is better than being in the ICU.

* * *

JULY 14, 1997

I still spend a lot of time napping. I'm exhausted from all the medication that is flowing through my body. I don't do much except lie in bed. I can't eat solid food, nor will I be able to for a while, so my meals consist of gelatin, pudding, and chicken broth. I really want a cheeseburger and fries, but that won't happen for quite some time since I won't be able to chew for a couple of months. When my grandparents come to visit, they go down to the cafeteria and buy me chocolate soft serve ice cream. Finally, something palatable!

My eyes have opened quite a bit more so I can actually see what's in front of me now. The swelling hasn't receded completely, but I can see enough to watch TV and see my family. The nurses make their routine visits to check my vitals, but otherwise they leave us alone. Someone does, however, come by in the middle of the night a few times to clear my lungs. A nurse sits me upright and gives me a mask to place over my nose and mouth. As I breathe in the oxygen, the nurse cups her hands and slaps my back over and over. This breaks up the mucus in my lungs, but I hate it. It doesn't hurt at all, it's not even really uncomfortable, but it's a reminder that I'm in the hospital. Breathing oxygen from a mask always reminds me of the moments before a surgery when I'm lying on the operating table about to fall asleep. And now I know I'm going to hate when people slap me on the back, too, because it will bring me back to this time and place. I dread the nighttime here because I just want the nurses to leave me alone. I don't sleep through the night, but I don't want them to come in to bother me either way. I can't wait to go home. I wonder when that will happen.

At least if I am stuck in this hospital, I can have visitors. I've had quite a few people stop by over the last few days, which reminds me I am loved. My mom's friends from work come down, our bartender friends from T.G.I. Friday's stop by to see how I am doing, and my friend Monica surprises me with a visit. Maybe it's because my other surgeries happened while I was still a young kid, but I have never had a friend my age visit me in the hospital. I can't explain how much this means to me. She doesn't pity me in my current state. Instead, she urges me to heal. For the first time, I actually want to get out of the bed and walk the halls of the hospital. My mom asks the nurses for a wheelchair and then helps me out of bed. I'm fragile, too fragile. My brand-new pajama pants are already falling off my hips. My liquid diet has taken its toll on my body, but we don't dwell on that now. I slowly and cautiously sit in the wheelchair, and Monica begins to push me up and down the hallway. It feels so freeing to sit in this chair and have a change of scenery, even if it is just sterile hallways.

After everyone leaves, my mom helps me on the scale located just outside of my room. I have lost twelve pounds in the last five days. I'm fourteen years old and under one hundred pounds now. I'm skin and bones. But this won't last. Nothing but the memories stick with me for long.

* * *

July 15, 1997

I'm going home today! It's been a rough week and I understand the healing process won't be over for a while. I'm still swollen, but I know I've been through a lot. It'll be interesting to see what my face looks like in a few months.

The nurse comes to remove the IV and I feel as if I am no longer a prisoner in this place. As soon as my release paperwork is signed and someone brings up a wheelchair, we can head home to Boca Raton. My life at home will be similar to here for a while. I'll watch television on the couch and nap all day long. I'll need help moving around the house and bathing. I won't be able to chew my food until my bones fully heal, which is at least two months, so I'll be on a diet of anything soft and mushy. Even though I won't be back to life pre-surgery for a while, I'm perfectly content healing in the comfort of my own home. As I mentioned, this is my life, my normal. It's all I've ever known.

As much as I love watching people celebrate their uniqueness, there are times I avoid my own at all costs. If I'm urged to share the stage with others who hold similar life experiences, I momentarily lose interest in being a gladiator for self-acceptance. It becomes both a reminder that far too many of us share similar struggles and a realization that my hardships pale in comparison to some others. For example, the severity spectrum for Treacher Collins syndrome ranges anywhere from barely noticeable deformities to being considered essentially born without a face. Despite any number of surgeries, the life of someone with a severe case of TCS may never skim the surface of normalcy. There is no way I can compare my story to theirs, even though I have my fair share of battle scars.

Despite our possible differences, I often feel that if I associate with other people who have craniofacial anomalies, I might create bonds I am uncomfortable forming. Our commonality might force me to address issues I would rather avoid.

Since I was raised in a nurturing community, it wasn't every day I saw myself as different from my classmates or friends. I was raised to focus on all the ways I fit in with society, not how I stood out. Though I knew my life was a bit outside the box, my upbringing shielded me from being some bully's verbal punching bag. In some ways, I still very much enjoy the naïveté attached to forgetting that my life has been less than normal.

Because of these realizations, I often hesitate before opening my mind to experiences centered around facial abnormalities. In the spring of 1999, Dr. Wolfe mentioned that a local couple had started a weekend summer camp for families with children with cranio-facial anomalies. Though I was now a teenager, he thought I would like to attend camp that summer to offer support to families in situations similar to mine. His comments passed straight through my hearing aid without stopping for consideration. I had recently undergone two operations in a two-month span to lengthen my jaw, an excruciating process. At that moment, the last thing I wanted was to spread optimism to children who might someday experience the same agonizing procedure. I wanted to concentrate on anything other than my syndrome. I wanted to forget the last two months, not relive them. So I did not attend the camp.

The following year, my doctor mentioned this camp again. At first, I was uninterested. If I attended, I would be acknowledging my flaws and even drawing attention to them, something I wasn't comfortable doing. Part of me again wanted to say no. I thought of all the ways in which surrounding myself with children similarly situated to me would force me to abandon the course of normalcy I'd been treading. While my syndrome did dictate certain aspects of my life, it never made me feel any less confident than my peers, nor did I ever encounter a desire to reach out to other Treacher Collins patients for moral support. I didn't need to.

When I was two, my mom took me to a support and play group for children with disabilities, but instantly she could tell I didn't belong. I was far too advanced in my development, and I acted as if I didn't have a different bone in my body. We never returned for round two.

Aside from when I looked in the mirror, caught other people staring at me, or visited the hospital, I felt utterly ordinary. Attending this camp would only serve to remind me that I really wasn't. I never pretended to be better than anyone else who had my condition, and that certainly wasn't the reason I avoided being in group situations with them. It's just that it was harder for me to actually confront my own reality than it was to silently deal with it and move on.

Despite these natural aversions, I set aside the judgments I found myself making and accepted my situation. I decided I would, and should, attend the next camp in hopes of helping younger children with facial abnormalities navigate their early years. I recognized that not everyone grew up surrounded by the same level of love, hope, and encouragement that I did. It was my duty to step outside my comfort zone and act as an inspiration to others for once.

The anxiety one feels when starting a new school was exactly what coursed through my veins on the drive down to Camp Super Nova that June day. I feared this unknown, but my parents taught me never to back down from a commitment. As the car pulled into the parking lot of the local college, a lump rose in my throat. I had reached the point of no return.

I schlepped my bedding, towel, and duffel bag of clothes through the double doors of the college dormitory where we would all be staying. Smiling faces immediately greeted and welcomed me. Neither the organizers of this camp nor the volunteers (many of whom were high school students) displayed any visible signs of facial differences, but I instantaneously knew they cared about those who did.

As the children and their families arrived, it became evident that we created a united front. Everyone who entered into the lobby of the dormitory came searching for a place they could blend in and find comfort. I met children with Crouzon syndrome, another disfiguring anomaly, and cleft palates. Some wore metal halos around their heads from recent jaw surgeries; others sported over-the-head, bone-conduction hearing aids like mine. Because of their abnormal facial formations, a handful of the children had difficulty speaking clearly. Here, though, none of that mattered.

What I hadn't realized when I agreed to this weekend was that for the first time ever I would be entering a completely judgment-free zone. That was a new scenario for me. Yes, my friends and family offered that same environment on a daily basis; however, strangers did not practice the same level of nonchalance and acceptance toward my physical appearance. Every attendee of the camp associated himself or herself with an anomaly in some capacity, whether that person was the child with the syndrome, a sibling, or a parent. There wasn't a single person that weekend who didn't show love and compassion. Because everyone dealt with something similar, I noticed none of the double-takes, sideways glances, or finger-pointing I was accustomed to from the outside world.

This camp achieved a vital level of unexpected comfort I never realized I'd missed. It offered a place of solace and connection by showing these children (and me) they weren't alone in dealing with their uncommon situations. It allowed them to run free without fear of harassment. It became a safe haven of sorts, like the X-Mansion in *X-Men*, where all of us with mutated genes could gather and live without persecution.

Prior to this weekend, I had met only one other person with Treacher Collins syndrome, and that had happened outside the elevator of my reconstructive surgeon's office. As my mom and I left a routine post-operation appointment, another mother brought her child to see Dr. Wolfe. As the elevator doors opened and the pair stepped into the hallway, the other mother seemingly realized her daughter had a companion in her struggle with TCS. She smiled and became animated, and then she excitedly asked me for the opportunity to take a photo of her daughter and me, two peas in a pod.

Contrary to what I had encountered in the outside world, at Camp Super Nova I experienced a kind of sensory surge when I saw so many people with facial anomalies. It was so uplifting. Almost before I could find my dorm room for the weekend, the organizers of the camp introduced me to several individuals with Treacher Collins: a young boy and his mother, a middle-school-aged boy, and another grown woman. If you do a web search for "Treacher Collins syndrome," you'll find photos of people who look eerily similar, no matter their race, gender, or age. If you know the characteristics, it's easy to discern who has this syndrome. The five of us appeared to be related, and even in a place overrun with anomalies, people questioned whether we actually were family.

I bonded with the other four and their families from the moment we met. We clung to each other, not out of necessity, but because of the deeply rooted connection we all had. I heard stories of the struggles the boys faced at school, and I agonized with them. Yet I found hope for my own future after hearing that the grown woman was getting married soon. And, among the more mundane-yet-great things I experienced was that if one of our hearing aid batteries lost its juice and we had forgotten to bring more, someone else had an entire pack at the ready.

The few days I spent with this group of people felt more like a vacation with friends than a gathering of people with abnormalities. Though the organizers did provide separate sessions for the children and parents on how to handle their unique situations, the camp largely focused on kids simply being kids in a welcoming and nurturing atmosphere. The organizers offered encouraging platforms for everyone to share their talents, whether that was singing, acting, or dancing. They welcomed diversity and fostered acceptance. This truly was a weekend for families to realize they weren't alone, for kids to be kids free of fear and hesitation, and for parents to find support they might not have known they needed.

I returned to the camp the following two summers and brought along a different friend each time. On my first visit to the camp, I stayed in the background alongside my Treacher Collins posse, reluctant to take an active role in activities. By the next year, however, I upped the ante and actively participated as a counselor when needed. With the help of my best friend, Lisa, we organized a skit and dance for a group of children to perform on the last day of camp.

That second year I also dove into the more significant aspects of the weekend by sitting on the panel of the parents' sessions. Those of us up front came from all walks of life and presented different viewpoints of our situations. Some of the parents with younger children struggled with the notion of operations. Should they or shouldn't they send their kids into these harrowing situations? Would it be necessary? Their children protested the hospital visits, and as parents, they hated forcing their kids into the operating room.

When it came time for me to offer up my own beliefs on the values of surgeries, I told the parents that even though their children would protest, those surgeries would prove to be life-changing in the grand scheme of things. Of course, no parent wants to see his or her child lying incapacitated in the intensive care unit strapped to a respirator. My own parents told me that was heart-wrenching for them. But I explained to the audience that one day they would look back at even the worst of surgeries with equanimity and think of it as nothing more than a distant memory, a minor nuisance that passed long ago; the positive effects from the surgeries would be long-lasting and life-altering. I gave this advice despite how I'd reacted a few years prior when I found out I'd have an operation after a seven-year hiatus. Today, though, I couldn't possibly imagine who I would be or what kind of life I would have if my parents had relented.

Those parents needed to understand the importance of remaining in control of their children's situations. Operations may not have been a solution for everyone, but no matter how many negative memories I accumulated over my years of surgeries, my life could have played out much differently without them. Though at times I seemed forced into those circumstances, I understood my parents' good intentions.

Each weekend I spent at Camp Super Nova, I left feeling accomplished, accepted, and whole. Accomplished, because I knew my words and my story brought hope to others as they faced trying circumstances, and hope was something hard to find in the outside world. Accepted, because I never once had to face curious eyes straining to see what I looked like. And whole, because though I never felt I required it, I found comfort in bonding with people who shared my daily experiences.

I entered the first weekend at camp clinging to the belief that this environment would cause me to be more aware of my condition, and it did. But simultaneously it allowed me to view the world as I always wanted it to view me: unlimited, carefree, and unaffected.

Camp Super Nova was an experience I truly cherished, and it contributed greatly to my growth and maturity as an individual.

FEBRUARY 16, 1999

It's the middle of my sophomore year of high school, and Dr. Wolfe wants to do a two-part procedure to lengthen my jaw. It seems pretty simple. He will insert some sort of device to help with this process during today's operation, and then in a few months, he'll remove it. I'm not too worried about the whole process. It doesn't seem like it's that big of a deal compared to the jaw surgery I had two years ago. Of course, I still have butterflies in my stomach as I wait to be taken back into the operating room, but when I wake up, I should be able to see what's going on around me and wear my hearing aid. Everything just seems more bearable with this. I'm just sorry I have to miss a week of school and a week of practice for the school musical!

Waking up in the recovery room after my surgery, I don't feel too awful. As predicted, I can see and hear, which is an unusual feeling after an operation. I'm definitely a bit swollen in the jaw area, but it doesn't really bother me. But I do notice something that freaks me out. I have two metal pieces that resemble screws sticking out underneath my chin. What the heck are these?! I was told that this entire contraption would be hidden somehow. Now I feel like some kind of freak made partially of metal.

I'm told that because of the small size of my mouth, the surgeon couldn't place the device entirely inside. I guess this is still better than having the completely external device, where the entire contraption would surround my head like a halo, but I still wasn't expecting this. It'll take me a while to get used to having metal protruding from my body, and I'm sure it will cause more kids to stare at me. It won't be forever, though. If this is the worst part of the process, I'll survive.

As soon as the anesthesia wears off, the nurses transfer me from the recovery room to my own private hospital room. This is great! My family can come visit if they want and not worry about being too loud, and I can watch television in the middle of the night if I can't sleep.

Feeling this vibrant and mobile after an operation is completely foreign to me. It's still the day of my operation and I'm not required to lie in bed like a slug. Of course, I shouldn't overexert myself, but if I have to go to the bathroom, I can walk to the toilet and not rely on a bedpan. Trust me, once you pee lying down, you appreciate toilets a lot more.

My mom tells me my grandparents are driving down to the hospital to see me. She helps me out of bed so I can go to the bathroom before they get here, but as soon as I start to walk, I urinate on the hospital room floor. What just happened? I seem to have absolutely no control over my bladder, and that disturbs me a little. My mom assures me everything will return to normal, but after the second time I fail to reach the bathroom, I worry I'll need to start wearing adult diapers. My body eventually regains control over its everyday functions, and I quickly return to thinking this entire procedure isn't so horrible.

* * *

FEBRUARY 17, 1999

It's been an easy day. I can't explain how amazing it has been to see and hear everything that's going on around me. I fed myself this morning, and I actually saw what I was eating. I never understood the beauty of something so simple, but after all my past operations, it's a joy to be this aware of my surroundings so soon after surgery. I'll be on another liquid diet again until this jaw contraption is removed. My orthodontist will be wiring my mouth shut in a few days using thick rubber bands. This will help my bones heal in a certain way. I'm not really sure what that will be like, but I bet it won't be horrible. Again, I've dealt with worse, and I've already been on a soft-food diet, so I know I can handle it for a couple of months.

A hospital stay is never pleasant, but this one is pretty easy. I should be discharged tomorrow. I'm definitely not looking forward to coming back in a couple months, though, but I'll try not to think about it.

Kid–Free Zone

My tumultuous past heavily dictated my views on the future. For one thing, I decided long ago I would never have children. I could not imagine my child enduring the same kind of suffering I experienced during my younger years. This notion was only reinforced by the time I spent at Camp Super Nova. I heard numerous parents relaying stories about the torment their children suffered as a result of their physical deformities. Their sad stories seemingly overshadowed any pleasurable moments they experienced as parents. I have to admit that their stories even took some of the luster off the many positive experiences I encountered during my early life. I began to wonder if my own parents felt the same way about me. Was I a burden to my parents the way these people said their children were to them?

I always hear people say they don't care about the gender of their unborn baby, as long it's healthy. That statement infuriates me. The very thing these people dread as soon-to-be parents happened to mine. Their baby girl wasn't born healthy. I'm sure my parents wished for a perfectly healthy child, but a Treacher Collins baby came along instead. My problems weren't life-threatening, but they were still problems. I wasn't the picture-perfect newborn they thought they were going to have. I wasn't the model of health. But they loved me just the same, as any decent parent in that situation would. For that I am truly grateful.

I don't expect anyone to stop saying those awful words, because they are true. Everybody wants to have healthy babies. But I do ask not to be judged when I say that I don't ever want to have my own children. My chances of delivering a healthy baby are at best fifty percent. Those are the odds of people with Treacher Collins syndrome passing along the defective gene to their offspring. It's a common concern for people like me. As with anything in life, we don't all agree on the same course of action. Some will confidently try to bear children despite the risk; others will not.

I refuse to be the root of a genetic defect. I know that sounds harsh, but I refuse to willingly cause another human being to have a life of pain and torment. As a mother, I would relate to my children too much; I would have to relive and share their suffering.

The insecurities associated with an anomaly are manageable; I have demonstrated that. And almost certainly, any child of mine probably would find some imperfections in her appearance, even if she didn't have a disability. But if she did, the years of being cut open, sewn shut, and left swollen beyond belief would take their toll on her, as well as on me. I know the fear and pain all too well. I would not want my child to live that kind of life. Despite the fact that I was surrounded by constant love and acceptance, I will not willingly bring into this world a life that might endure the same painful procedures I once did. It wouldn't be fair, and I cannot do that to my child.

Of course, if I did have a child, there would be multiple possibilities for the outcome. She might not carry the mutated gene at all; she might only display a minimal case of TCS; or she might have a very severe case and be born without any facial features whatsoever. The wide severity spectrum presents no clues on just how much an unborn child will be affected. And even though I would be able, nowadays, to test my child in utero for the gene associated with TCS, the results would not divulge the severity of the syndrome if the syndrome were found. In any case, if the gene were spotted, it would do only one of two things: prepare me for having a child with a facial anomaly, or allow me to investigate releasing her for adoption if I felt emotionally or financially unable to keep her. After thirty-three years of living with Treacher Collins myself, mentally preparing for it would not be necessary. I'm quite equipped to handle that scenario. And obviously, putting my child up for adoption because of her mutation would make me the biggest hypocrite on the face of the earth. So in my case, genetic testing would be a complete waste of time.

My desire to avoid passing along my Treacher Collins gene stems from my first-hand knowledge of the condition, not from fear. Because of that, I determined never to tempt fate and to avoid a pregnancy if at all possible. If I truly want a child in the future, I will adopt. The world holds a plethora of children desperately searching for loving homes. My connection to my child would not diminish because our DNA doesn't overlap. I think the bond potentially could grow stronger, knowing that I chose to save a life, not just create a life.

My lack of wanting children, biological or otherwise, isn't completely selfless, though. Kids terrify me, plain and simple. Their openness and honesty lead to unfiltered comments, which I am not always in the frame of mind to accept. They speak only the truth because they have not yet learned the art of lying. Sometimes, the truth hurts.

Because children have always been the primary people ogling at my physical appearance, they make me squirm. Not everyone enjoys children, for various reasons, and I happen to be one of those people. I have more patience for teenagers than for toddlers, for the elderly in Depends than for babies in Pampers, for a houseful of barking dogs than for a houseful of whining kids. I wasn't meant for babysitting, let alone motherhood.

Over the years, especially when I was younger, I received many inquisitions of, "What happened to your face?" A quizzical furrow of the brow and a blank expression always accompanied this question. And often times, the child spoke these words with an undertone of disgust. At least, after repeatedly hearing the same query, that's how I've grown to interpret it. "What's that?" they would remark, commenting on my hearing aid while pointing at it. "Why are your ears so small?" they would interrogate with squinted eyes and a cocked head. And to the ones who asked those questions, I answered honestly, even if they unnerved me. "I was born like this." "This is a hearing aid. It helps me hear the same way glasses help you see." "I have a syndrome. Do you know what a syndrome is?" What else could I do? I've always urged people to ask me questions, so I couldn't mock these children for doing exactly what I preferred they do instead of staring or laughing at my deformity.

Even still, it's hard for me to face new children, uncertain how they will respond to my appearance. Now that I am older and my face has transformed into something less unique after all my surgeries, I shouldn't harbor such worries, but habit forbids me from forgetting the distress of my youth. If I know I'll be spending the day with my friends and meeting their kids for the first time, I'll consider leaving my hair down and wearing sunglasses all day. This hides my facial scars, malformed ears, and hearing aid. By creating a natural disguise, I mask my flaws. But as quickly as that thought enters my mind, it exits. My friends understand the sensitivity I feel toward children and their reactions. They tell their kids ahead of time about my differences. They teach them to be accepting of everyone from the get-go. And when my friends finally introduce us, their kids have been prepared to receive my abnormalities without hesitation.

If every parent took the same measures to teach proper social behavior, I might have adopted a more unguarded approach to motherhood, and to children in general. Unfortunately, not every parent embodies the same values, and children base their reactions on what they learn from watching their parents.

My family brought me to a playground one day when I unsuspectingly walked too close to an older Caucasian girl confused by my uncommon facial features. When I encroached on her personal space, she responded with, "I don't like her face." My father explained to her, "Not everybody looks the same, but she's a nice girl just like you." The girl then replied, "I don't like her. She's a n***er." I've always abhorred that word; even as a child, I knew its cruel intent. When someone directed it toward me, I gained an even greater appreciation of how hurtful and painful it is. The only way she could have learned such a malicious word—and grasped its malevolent nature—was from overhearing it at home, no doubt in a negative situation.

My dad immediately told her about the severity of that word and that she should never refer to anyone that way. The girl responded dismissively. "So? I don't care. She's still a n***er!"

What followed next was not my dad's proudest moment. He acted out of raw emotion, anger, and hurt. "Well, you're a n***er," he said to her.

"No, I'm not!"

"Yes, you are."

"I'm going to tell my dad what you said!" she cried as she ran off to find her own father. My dad glared in his direction with revulsion beaming from his eyes, hoping the stranger would come over to confront him. My father would have some choice words for him. As his daughter relayed the incident, her father stared quizzically at us but did not venture over. The incident was diffused. Sticks and stones.

Children soak up information, phrases, and behavior like sponges. I undoubtedly would raise any child of mine to hold the same values my parents instilled in me. I know my child would love and accept me with my flaws, as I would her, but I've spent too many years under the microscopic eyes of children to find the novelty of offspring appealing. It's a personal choice to remain childless, but it's a path I happily accept.

APRIL 29, 1999

Holy crap! I grossly underestimated the last two months. I didn't mind having my mouth wired shut. I learned to speak like a ventriloquist without moving my jaw. I didn't even mind the meals of pureed food. I still can't wait to sink my teeth into a juicy burger, but my mom did the best she could to ensure my mushed-up meals were tasty. What bothered me most was the actual lengthening process of the jaw. That was the most horrific and painful experience of my life.

During the first procedure, Dr. Wolfe broke my jaw and secured a metal device to either side of the fracture. This device, known as a distractor, was adjusted on a daily basis so that the crack in my jaw would be increased after each adjustment. This process slowly lengthened my lower jaw and eventually eliminated my receding chin—and it was excruciating to endure. I've never been more grateful to be having an operation. I want this distraction device out of my jaw right now. Right now!

I'm not even thinking about the state I'll be in after the operation. Dr. Wolfe is doing more than simply removing the device; he will be implanting cartilage grafts from my rib into my chin and cheekbones, and cleaning up the incisions underneath my lower eyelids. I asked for a rhinoplasty, too, since I hate the shape of my nose. I'm most looking forward to that, actually.

* * *

After my surgery, I am taken to the intensive care unit, still intubated through my nose. Once again I cannot see because my eyes are swollen shut. God, I hate this feeling. I'm helpless and so reliant on everyone else around me. I have to trust these people whom I can't even see. I continue to drift in and out of consciousness because of the pain medication.

* * *

APRIL 30, 1999

I'm now lying here in the ICU, not really thinking of anything. My thoughts are so jumbled and blurry that it's hard to concentrate on anything. I don't really know what time of day it is. It could be the middle of the night. I just kind of exist here. The nurses come over to tell me they are going to change my bedding. I try to mumble OK, but I realize no sound is coming from my lips. I know I can't speak well right now, but I was able to answer simple questions earlier. Why can't I say anything now?

The nurses roll my body onto its right side. Why do I feel so limp? This is strange. They roll me over on to my left side. What is wrong with me? I try to speak, but nothing comes out. My lips don't even move. I try to wiggle my fingers, toes, arms, and legs, but I literally have lost control of my body. I realize I'm paralyzed. I'm aware of everything happening, but I can't move or speak. I can't communicate at all. Does anyone even know what's happening? Why am I paralyzed? Oh God! Where is my mom? I want my mom! Of course, I can't tell anyone that, because I can't speak! I fall back to sleep wondering what happened and if I'm permanently immobile.

The next time I wake up, I realize my bladder feels too full. This shouldn't happen. I have a catheter in place so I don't have to worry about going to the bathroom. But why in the world does my bladder feel so full? Of course, I can't really tell anyone this, because I still can't move or speak. Oh my God, I think I'm going to have a heart attack at sixteen because I am so stressed out. I'm surrounded by medical professionals, yet I feel completely alone and powerless. If I can't explain to them what is happening, how are they supposed to help me?

I lose consciousness again for who knows how long. My mom is back now. I try everything in my power to say something to her, and I manage to tell her I have to pee. The immobility is wearing off. I'm beginning to gain speech back.

"Honey, you have a catheter in. You can go," she tells me. I muster up all the strength I can to point to the area, and I must have moved my finger because she lifts up the sheets and repositions my leg. And suddenly, my bladder begins to empty. I had been lying on the catheter tube the whole time, which prevented me from urinating.

From everything I can remember, this is by far the worst post-op experience to date. I want my vision back, I want to transfer out of the ICU, but mostly, I just want to leave the hospital all together.

MAY 12, 1999

When I was moved into a regular hospital room, I realized I never had the rhinoplasty that I asked for. Because of the invasive work done to my jaw, Dr. Wolfe needed to intubate me through my nose instead of my mouth. He promised he would correct my nose in the future if I wanted, but that means another surgery. I'm not sure anymore.

I was discharged from the hospital on May 2, and I spent the next week recovering at home. I finally started back at school this past Monday, but today, Wednesday, I noticed a strange discharge coming from the incision on my chin. This is one of the places Dr. Wolfe implanted the rib graft. I immediately called my mom from school, and we are now at Miami Children's Hospital visiting with Dr. Wolfe in between his surgeries.

He takes a swab of the drainage and will send it to the lab with expedited results. He doesn't notice anything suspicious about the wound; there isn't any redness around the area. We're all hoping it's nothing serious like a staph infection. He prescribes an antibiotic just in case and tells me to come back to his office in two days.

* * *

MAY 14, 1999

I'm still draining a soupy liquid from my incision. Dr. Wolfe reviews the results of my culture, and I seem to have a yeast infection on my chin. Who knew that was even possible? He places me on antifungal medication and instructs me to continue with the antibiotic as well.

With all of my surgeries, I have never experienced a serious problem, but of course, there is always a risk. This could have been so much worse, but luckily, it seems I've made it through another surgery without any major setback or permanent damage. I wonder how many more times I'll have to worry about these nuances of my life. I'm sixteen. Am I done with surgeries yet?

The Nomadic Heart

My parents always hoped I would think back on my childhood with fondness and remember the positive elements rather than the hardships, and they did all they could to reinforce that. I had memorable birthday parties at places like the bowling alley and ice-skating rink; they allowed me to sleep over at friends' houses every weekend, if that's what I wanted; and they helped forge my passion for travel by taking me on trips across the United States.

Traveling represented a form of escape for me. It was everything I wanted in life: to be away from hospitals and doctors, to be away from school and teachers, and to be surrounded by loving people who cared only about my welfare. As strong as I appeared, I could handle my reality for only so long. There were moments when my life irritated me to such a degree that I felt I could not go on. It seemed as though all I ever did was visit doctors. I made the rounds that no one else had to: reconstructive surgeon, oral surgeon, maxillofacial surgeon, ophthalmologist, cornea specialist. At times, it was too much to bear, and I yearned to get away from it all. I had a very active imagination, which helped me cope on a day-to-day basis, but I needed something that would serve as a greater diversion. To be truly free, I needed to put physical distance between my real life and me. The best way to do that was by traveling. Not only was it fun, it became the best means possible to help me cope with the stresses of my situation.

I was never one to cling to a security blanket when I needed comforting. My safety net was a place, a place where I could fall into a moment of unwavering contentment. Walt Disney World opened me up to the endless possibilities of magic, fantasy, and imagination. It was a magical kingdom in which traveling the globe and dining with royalty were everyday occurrences. This was a world where I could be anything I ever wanted to be, no matter how outrageous my desires. But most important, I felt far removed from my reality the moment I entered the property. Riding underneath the welcome sign at Disney World and seeing that I had reached my happy place, I would breathe a sigh of relief, knowing that for a period of time I was in a perfect place where everyone was special, even a girl with all my problems.

Though only three hours north of my hometown, Disney World seemed light-years away. Each time we visited, my worries melted into pure nothingness. Reality faded into fantasy, and I concocted the notion that this magical world kept me safe. My parents brought me to Disney for my first visit when I was six months old. From that moment forward, we visited at least six times a year.

When he built this central Florida landmark, Walt Disney envisioned a place where people could escape everyday life. He wanted his guests to leave their struggles in the parking lot and enter into a place full of magic and wonder, a place where they could explore their imaginations without the weight of reality pushing down on them.

Everything Walt hoped to convey by creating Disney World, I experienced each time I crossed over the property line onto its grounds. Disney freed my mind of all troubles, even if only momentarily. These mind-clearing weekends became necessities. My parents would always promise a trip to Disney before a surgery, in order to contain my fear, and after a surgery, to reward my bravery. I valued these weekends because they provided a distraction from the upcoming operations and then served as a reminder that the difficult moments in my life didn't last forever.

We visited often enough that the characters began to recognize me. On one post-operation jaunt to Epcot, we saw Chip and Dale in the distance. Of course, I needed to go hug them and pose for pictures even though I had done so a month prior. As I walked up to where they stood, Chip spotted me, grabbed Dale's attention, and excitedly pulled him toward me, all the while ignoring the other children waiting patiently for their autographs. They remembered me from my visit prior to the surgery. At that moment, Chip and Dale made me feel like the most important child in Epcot. They eagerly dropped everything just to make my day special, and their magic worked. Moments like these freed me from myself.

My trips to Walt Disney World instigated my self-proclaimed gypsy soul. As I traveled more often, I realized it wasn't only a single place that soothed my nerves; any destination far enough away from my real life provided an escape. The grass grew greener wherever I journeyed, because nothing I dreaded was out there. There were no doctors, no hospitals, no needles, no transfusions. Those elements of my life receded in the rearview mirror when I was on the road.

I didn't worry about my problems when I traveled. In fact, I didn't worry about anything. I focused on the present, my surroundings, and the journey. I felt free, as if my Treacher Collins syndrome cut its reins and allowed me to roam and grow without my wondering what obstacle waited around the next corner. Each time I visited Colorado for a ski trip, I focused on the breathtaking mountains, the feeling of the snow beneath my skis, and the cool mountain air filling my lungs. I felt the most alive while I was on vacation because it allowed me to live without fear.

During my junior year in college, I jumped at the chance to study abroad in Florence, Italy. Never had I separated myself from my reality with that much distance. My nerves bubbled with both excitement and anxiety. I would be leaving the security of the familiar for the absolute unknown. What would life hold in those five months? How would the Italians respond to my facial abnormality? Would it even matter?

From the moment my plane touched down in Rome, I sensed a metamorphosis. Maybe my attention was misdirected by the beauty of the Eternal City or by the majesty of the Florentine Renaissance architecture, or maybe I was simply overwhelmed by being in a faraway place alone for the first time in my life, but one thing stood out as I ventured around Italy: Never did I catch even a single gaze from an Italian child. Never did I witness anyone slyly pointing in my direction while whispering to his friends. And perhaps because I didn't speak Italian well enough, but never did I hear a child questioning his parents about my misshapen ears or facial scarring. I did catch a copious amount of catcalls from men on the street, though. I guess in their minds, an American female was an American female, with or without a facial anomaly.

Whether the European culture embraced physical differences more openly than at home, or whether my eyes concentrated only on the unfamiliar, spectacular atmosphere I was experiencing, my mindset morphed into something more forgiving and pure. I dropped the edge I carried, the usual awareness that caused me to sense when curious eyes targeted my features. I truly forgot the emotional weight I lugged around daily. It all dissipated into the Italian air. For five glorious months, I existed as a whole, unaffected entity, mind, body, and soul. I was truly happy. Gallivanting across the globe allowed me to experience moments of perfection in my imperfect world.

It was in Florence that I discovered a little bit about myself that eased some of my spiritual pain. I learned that people are like works of art. Each has its own followers, its own lovers, and its own detractors. People, like art, are not all the same. Not everyone can appreciate the physical beauty of every person, just like they cannot appreciate the physical beauty of every piece of art. In my life, I know I am very much loved by many people—not just my parents—and that I have an inherent beauty that many people notice. But am I a Cellini masterpiece, a Botticelli work of perfection, or a Raphael tour de force? Perhaps not, but who is? There are very few people who can say they are beautiful enough to grace the covers of fashion magazines. That's why for me, as is true for almost everyone, it is up to others, as well as myself, to find and appreciate where my beauty lies.

But once I arrived back in the United States, my stable walls of self-assurance toppled to the ground. I found myself once again surrendering to my syndrome. It was bound to happen. I couldn't continue to pretend my Treacher Collins had magically healed itself while overseas. Life as it was pre-Italy resumed, but the memory of my complete transformation while I was away remained. Studying abroad, traveling to various countries whether alone or in a group—it all strengthened my nomadic heart.

Traveling became not only a way to escape the negatives in my life, but also a way to build on the positives. Today when I wander the unfamiliar streets of a new city, I reminisce about all the places I've been and look forward to the new experiences that will fill my life. But it doesn't really matter what I encounter, because all I truly care about is being away from home. That means no doctors, no hospitals, no transfusions, and no pain.

MAY 22, 2003

I wasn't expecting this surgery. The only reason I even agreed to it was because Dr. Wolfe still owes me a nose job. I know that sounds vain, but it was the only part of my last procedure that I actually wanted. I want this new nose for me, for my confidence, not because it's another symptom of my syndrome that needs correction. And so here I am, back in Miami Children's Hospital awaiting my next procedure.

It's crazy that I'm twenty years old, almost a junior in college, and still going to a children's hospital; but I'll come here as long as they accept me. The staff here is skilled, and they're used to treating odd cases like mine. I'm not sure an adult hospital would be comfortable intubating someone with a narrow trachea like I have. I hope I never have to find out either.

Along with the rhinoplasty, Dr. Wolfe will do more work to my cheeks and the area beneath my eyes. It seems like a never-ending process. He is happy with the amount of bone that has been placed in my cheeks over the years, but now he needs to continue to add tissue and fat for a more natural look. This time the incision on my hip will be reopened and dermal fat grafts will be transplanted to my cheeks. Just like when I was a child, he will cut an incision across my head and pull down the skin, revealing my bone structure. In some creepy, grotesque way, this process fascinates me. I really shouldn't think about it, though. I know it's dangerous to have my brain exposed like that, but I'm intrigued. I love learning, and I really don't want to focus on what can go wrong.

This is a relatively easy procedure for me because it's similar to so many of the surgeries I've had in the past. But I'm still nervous; of course I'm nervous. Who wouldn't be? But I know what to expect afterward. My head will be bandaged. My eyes will be swollen shut. I'll need help moving around the house and bathing. I won't say I'm thrilled about the operation, but there's a certain comfort in knowing what to expect after the fact. I'm just grateful to still be allowed at this children's hospital. It just adds to the familiarity of the whole procedure.

* * *

My surgery is finished, and Dr. Wolfe is discharging me! This is the best news ever! I really can't believe I don't have to spend the night in the hospital after everything my face just endured. I'm not complaining, though. I'll heal faster at home. My mom doesn't like it much because she will have to monitor my every move, but too bad for her. I'm going home! Where's the nurse? I want this IV out of my arm…STAT!

AUGUST 12, 2003

I've had the entire summer to heal, and now Dr. Wolfe wants to remove some tissue around my left eyelid before I head back to college. I know it's a simple office procedure, but the thought of being awake as he takes a scalpel to my face unnerves me. I thought my visits to this office were done for the summer, but I guess I was wrong.

My stomach churns as I lie on the reclining office chair. Someone sticks a needle in my face near my left eye. I can't tell who does this—maybe Dr. Wolfe, maybe his fellow, maybe a nurse. I don't even know who is in the room with me now. My eyes are closed and I'm trying to concentrate on something else, anything else. My junior year of college starts in a couple of weeks. I'm ready to see my friends. We're all living together this year.

"OK, Kristin. We're done," Dr. Wolfe says.

We're done? That's it? I was nervous for absolutely no reason. You'd think I'd be used to the unexpected by now, but I'm not. I don't think I will ever be. Oh well, time to go, I guess. I have a life to get back to.

Normal Scenarios, Abnormal Results

Though I walked through life believing I was utterly ordinary, I couldn't outrun my syndrome. People who didn't know me well referred to me by using my abnormalities as descriptors. To them I was the girl with the headset, the girl with the tiny ears, or the girl with the funny voice. My greatest insecurities became my easiest identifiers. I may have tried everything in my power to mask those flaws, but they were always the first things people noticed. Over time, those differences faded into familiarities, and people began referring to me by my name rather than my distinctive features.

Even if I didn't characterize myself by my syndrome, I couldn't deny its constant presence. My syndrome affected my everyday life. What seemed perfectly normal to me was completely foreign to everyone else. My hearing aid is a perfect example of that. It is critical to my existence; it serves as my salvation. It allows me to function normally by filling my muted world with sound.

An audiologist arranged to fit me for my over-the-head hearing aid when I was only six weeks old, and it has lasted thirty-three years. My little stubs of ears lacked ear holes, so the typical in-the-ear hearing aid was never an option. If I wanted to hear sound, I had to rely on bone conduction, a method that turned vibrations traveling through my cranium into sounds.

My hearing aid is attached to a wire, shaped to my head like a headband. On one end of the wire is the actual hearing aid, which takes in the sound. This is also where I can control the level of volume and change the battery. On the other end is the bone oscillator, which presses firmly against the skull bone and controls the vibrations. A chord wraps around the wire and connects the hearing aid to the oscillator, thus allowing sounds to flow from one end to the other.

The way I hear is nothing like someone with unobstructed ear canals. The oscillator picks up sound and amplifies it, causing vibrations against the skull. The cochleas then interpret these vibrations as sound. I can place the oscillator against any portion of my skull and hear the same level of noise. Because the entire skull absorbs the vibrations, sound doesn't have a distinctive starting point. I can't decipher the direction sounds come from; I just hear. If someone stands to my right and calls my name, I may turn full circle until I notice the person. My brain registers that someone is calling my name, but not the origin of the voice. I find this extremely frustrating. If I am out shopping with my mom and she calls for me ("Kristin! Kristin! Over here! Kristin! Over here!"), I spin around but am not able to trace her voice. I need directional cues in order to find her: "Kristin, stop. Now turn to your right."

No one realizes my level of hearing isn't natural, and up until recently, I didn't either. Because my hearing relies on vibrations against the bone that translate into a single overarching sound, my brain receives atypical signals. Only one sound amplifies at a time, whichever sound is most prominent. If someone talks to me, my brain picks up that speech more than the television in the background. If I'm in a noisy bar, I can't decipher individual conversations over the jumble of dialogues going on around me. I prefer to avoid such noisy, overly crowded environments because my inability to focus isolates me. If I can't decipher the words being said, I can't participate in the conversation. I end up sitting in silence lost in my own thoughts. I can't complain about how I hear, though; at least I hear. Bone conduction introduced amplified noise to my quiet world, and that's all that matters.

I own three total hearing aids, but I wear only one regularly, the one I've worn my entire life. Over the years, my head formed a slight depression from ear to ear created by the pressure the wire band exerted on my skull, but this depression serves as a perfect nesting place for the device. That hearing aid is so firmly in place that it sounds crisper and clearer than the other two. It might not produce natural hearing, but it's the best I have, and it provides my sense of normal hearing.

When these hearing aids eventually break—and they're bound to at some point—I cannot buy replacements. My archaic, over-the-head, bone-conduction hearing aids have been replaced with new technology. I first learned about these new, bone-anchored hearing aids from Dr. Wolfe when I was in my mid-twenties. During my annual appointment, he recommended I use one; however, he said it would require surgery. A titanium fixture would need to be implanted directly into the skull bone, which would protrude through the skin, serving as an anchor. This anchor resembles the bottom half of a snap. A sound processor then would clip on and off as needed. The hearing device has direct access to the skull. Because of this, skin doesn't obstruct the vibrations against the bone, and sound comes across as clearer and more natural.

I went back and forth about the idea of using this advanced hearing system. On one hand, my current hearing aid was well past its prime, and I thought that perhaps it was time I try the latest technology. On the other hand, the new system meant more surgery.

I asked my audiologist about the new anchored implants and she let me test one for a week. Because this was only a simulation of an actual device and not a true implant, the sound processor was attached to a wire and fit over my head, much like my bone-conduction hearing aid. There was no separate oscillator on this device, though. I chose to wear the hearing device with the sound processor pressed against the right side of my head. This was the location of the oscillator from my normal hearing aid, and I thought the pressure would feel familiar.

As soon as the audiologist activated the sound, I noticed the difference. I picked up every sound at once. I couldn't necessarily tell where the noises came from, but the effect was as though I was hearing in surround sound. I heard everything as being equally distinctive, something I had never done before, the effect of which was that I couldn't decipher what to focus on. My brain was in sensory overload. If this was natural hearing, I wasn't sure I wanted it. I even wore the device to work but couldn't focus on what I was doing. I couldn't drown out the background noise as I usually did. When my phone rang, I picked it up and pressed the receiver to my left ear, the same as I had always done. But my normal hearing aid wasn't there to capture the voice on the other end. I awkwardly shifted the phone to the sound processor on my right side and struggled to focus on the conversation. Weird. How do you break a lifelong practice, which was more of a necessity than a habit?

I wasn't convinced this new hearing implant would benefit me the same way it would a young child. I relied on a certain method of hearing, a certain sound I had long grown accustomed to. I was not afraid to learn something new, but this newness affected every moment of every day. For a week, I walked around feeling lost, making me realize that if I wanted this new hearing aid, I would have to learn how to hear all over again.

Would the implant be worth it? I debated the point in my mind. It would require undergoing another surgery, learning to hear in a whole new way, and permanently feeling self-conscious about having metal protruding through my skin. It's already awkward enough when I visit the hair salon and struggle to keep up with the conversation with my stylist. How would I feel when the girl washing my hair saw this exposed metal snap? I didn't feel like adding another explanation to my already long list of Treacher Collins topics.

The more I thought about it, the more I realized this implant wouldn't just affect my hearing. I wouldn't be able to wear my sunglasses or other things that normally rest on the ears. With my bone-conduction aid, my glasses fit stably on top of the oscillator and hearing aid box. I wouldn't have that with the implant. I would then need prosthetic ears, which would include more surgery. That, coupled with the exposed metal from the anchor, made my decision easy. An implant would spiral into something much more. I refused to change that much about myself if I didn't have to. My archaic devices worked well enough. I decided not to alter my sense of normal just so I could function more like everyone else.

The use of a hearing aid is my normal. I flit between two different worlds: sound and silence. I wear my hearing device throughout the day but remove it to sleep, shower, or swim. I suddenly leave a world where birds chirp outside, music plays on the radio, and waves crash in the ocean. When I remove my hearing aid, I enter a realm of nothingness. At night, when I fall asleep, I shut my eyes and feel entirely untouchable. As a little girl, I felt that monsters under my bed couldn't hurt me because at that moment I didn't exist. The world was both dark and silent.

This worked to my benefit in college. I could sleep even if someone nearby held a raging party. When my roommates wanted to stay awake to watch television or talk, I turned off the sound and went to sleep. I considered the silence soothing. It allowed me to tune out the outside world, whereas others didn't have that luxury. I could lie in bed at night and let my imagination wander without interruption.

Living in this silence wasn't without its disadvantages, though. While I usually enjoyed uninterrupted sleep, there were certain instances when I knew I needed to be awakened, and noise was the only way to do that. For instance, if I had an early-morning meeting that required that I get up before my normal wake-up time; if someone broke into my house and I needed to take action; or if a fire erupted and I had to evacuate the building. How could I wake up to a clock alarm, a fire alarm, or a burglar alarm if I couldn't hear them?

I didn't start using an alarm to wake up until I studied abroad in Italy. Before then, my parents always woke me for school by using my other senses: sight and touch. They either turned on my bedroom light or patted my back to ease me into consciousness. In the first years of college, I relied heavily on my internal alarm. My earliest classes never started before nine in the morning. The tiniest sliver of the sun rising in the morning would wake me instantly. But in Italy, I needed an alarm to wake me because I had to be up before dawn. I used my cell phone for that purpose. I set the alarm to some obnoxious sound and turned up the volume to the highest setting. Before knowing that I could rely on it, however, I had to see if it would work.

As a test one day, I turned off my hearing aid and played the sound from the cell phone alarm. I could hear it in the distance but wasn't sure it would be loud enough to jolt me from a deep sleep. I was concerned about that because during my freshman year in college, I slept through a fire alarm that went off during the night, and my roommate had to shake me to rouse me from my sleep. On another occasion, I didn't hear the blaring house alarm my cousin set off when she sleepwalked downstairs and triggered the motion sensor. If those deafening sirens didn't stir me, how could I expect the subtle horn from my cell phone to do so?

The first time I had to wake up with an alarm, I placed the phone next to my head while I slept, hoping the close proximity to my ears would allow me to hear it. I had a fitful sleep that night, and worry made me toss and turn. At the scheduled time, however, my alarm sounded and I jerked awake, as did my roommate, much to her dismay. I didn't care, though. I could hear my alarm. It worked. It really worked.

My hearing aid is a perfect example of the way in which I have to adapt to ordinary occurrences in life. I live in a world full of slight modifications, where typical situations require that I take atypical paths to reach the same results. But I usually move so effortlessly through life that people don't realize the daily challenges I actually face. I need to think before I act, whereas others do things casually, without fear of repercussions.

If I decide to go into town with my friends and we get caught in the rain, I worry that my hearing aid might be ruined. If I play sports and a ball or other object strikes my eye, I worry that my transplanted cornea might become unstable. If I sit in the front seat of a car, I worry that if we get into an accident, the air bag will deploy and fracture my facial bones. I cannot ignore these nagging concerns. If I do, and something happens, I can unravel years of work with one foolish action. That's why, for example, even to this day I prefer to sit in the back seat of a car when I'm with a group of people.

I'd love to be free from these worries. I'd love to know what sound the water makes as it hits my head in the shower. This is something I'll never experience because my hearing aid can't get wet. Just once I'd love to run through the rain without an umbrella and still be aware of the sounds around me. I'd love to relax in a pool while wearing my hearing aid and not worry about someone accidentally splashing my head.

I'd give anything to enjoy my time spent at a water park without the struggle of interpreting what everyone around me says. I find myself caught between two worlds. One moment, when my hearing aid is on, I'm engaged in conversations going on around me, and the next, when I'm forced to take it off, I'm fighting to make sense of muffled voices. It's surreal watching everyone else around me interact with ease while I require complete focus. I fight the frustration of floating between sound and silence, of being in a world where my hearing allows me to fit in, and then cross over into a world where I feel small and alone. I use my hearing aid as a bridge to normalcy. Without it, I feel insignificant. I have no other way to interact with the world around me.

Though my hearing loss largely contributed to the unusual way I handled many typical situations, it wasn't the only reason that I was forced to alter my approach to certain aspects of my life. I suffered from severe tension in my neck that wouldn't go away. After months of suffering from this, I decided to visit a chiropractor. Numerous friends received frequent adjustments and raved about the results. I was tired of living in pain and decided to heed their advice.

I met with the chiropractor and told him about my numerous facial reconstruction surgeries. I made the mistake of glossing over my jaw surgeries. I suppose I thought the severity of those surgeries was implied. I sometimes forget that people—even medical professionals—aren't familiar with Treacher Collins syndrome, let alone the complexities behind it. The chiropractor first instructed me to lie on my stomach so he could adjust my spine. Then I flipped over onto my back, and he positioned his hands around my jaw and skull to crack the neck. I walked out of the office after my adjustment feeling the tension begin to disappear. Later that day though, I was chewing on pumpkin seeds and my jaw suddenly began to pop, like it had dislodged. It hurt to open my mouth and chew. What had I done? I mentioned this to the chiropractor on my next visit, and as much as he tried to realign the jaw, the damage had been done. The pain eventually subsided and the popping lessened, but it has never returned to normal. I now understand the importance of being specific. I can't afford not to be. I no longer assume what works for everyone else will work for me, because there are aspects of my life that only I understand. This incident now forces me to evaluate how certain situations might affect my life before I act, even if no one else has to do the same.

It is not only my facial anomalies that force me to assess my specific concerns, but other conditions as well. In 2006, I underwent a cornea transplant because of my keratoconus. Two years later, I developed pink eye, a very common problem. I found a cornea specialist in my neighborhood who had never treated me before, and he gave me steroid drops to help my eye heal. It seemed to work, and I thought nothing else of it. Two weeks later, I noticed that the vision in my right eye had become hazy and sensitive to light. I assumed the pink eye had returned. I contacted the ophthalmologist who had performed my cornea transplant, and he referred me to another cornea specialist in my area. That doctor told me something that devastated me. He said I wasn't suffering from pink eye. Instead, after two years, my body was rejecting my transplanted cornea. I was terrified. I was told at the time of my cornea transplant that I faced the possibility of corneal rejection, but I also was told that rejection usually happened within the first year after the surgery.

I sat in the chair awaiting my fate, wondering if the rejection could be reversed. If not, I probably would need another transplant. But if I tried again, could I force my body to accept another donor cornea? If the first transplant didn't work, what assurances did I have that the second one would work? I was so afraid of losing my vision.

Fortunately, my new ophthalmologist put me on an aggressive treatment of steroid drops, and the rejection soon subsided—another disaster averted in my complex and unusual life. My vision returned, but I am now reminded of my transplant each night as I squeeze one drop of a liquid steroid into my eye. I'll continue to do this my entire life to actively prevent another rejection. This comes with risks. The overuse of steroids can build up the pressure in my eye, leading to serious issues such as glaucoma. Because of this, I visit my eye doctor every six months. Recently, my pressure did rise too high and I felt my eye begin to tighten. My doctor stopped the steroid application until the pressure dropped to a normal level.

As long as I live, I'll face the fear of cornea rejection. It could happen at any time, no matter how many years pass since the transplant. That scares me, but I don't dwell on it. I continue to use a lower-dosage steroid and hope for the best. What else can I do?

I feel as though I'll never experience the ordinary moments most people take for granted. I'll never hear unassisted or shower in anything other than silence. I'll always worry that the slightest irregularity in my vision might be a sign that my body no longer accepts my donor cornea. But this is my life, and these irregularities are all I've ever known. It's my sense of normal, and I've come to accept it.

OCTOBER 28, 2005

This has been the week from hell. First, something happened with my insurance and I had to postpone my scheduled surgery. Next, Hurricane Wilma swept over South Florida, leaving my family's house without power, a broken window in one of the bedrooms, and very few options for gasoline for the car. My mom and I had to drive an hour down to Miami yesterday for my pre-operation registration, and we hoped to find an open gas station somewhere along the way. Lastly, my nerves are shot, because for the first time, my operation isn't at Miami Children's Hospital. Dr. Wolfe pushed for the surgery to be held there, but I'm too old now.

I'm twenty-two and a fresh college graduate. I wasn't sure what I wanted to do after graduation, so I opted for the one constant thing in my life: a surgery. At this very moment, I regret that decision. I'm lying in a foreign hospital wondering if the staff can even handle my case.

I'm seriously a ball of nerves. I hate this feeling. The anesthesiologist comes to introduce himself, and my mom explains how difficult it is to intubate me. They continue talking about my experiences at Miami Children's Hospital, but I tune them out.

Breathe, Kristin. Just breathe. Everything is going to be fine.

The anesthesiologist comes back after some time. Truthfully, I didn't realize he had even left in the first place. He says he spoke with my former anesthesiologist and feels comfortable now. He hands me a mask to put over my face and tells me to breathe deeply for a few minutes. This will numb my trachea and make the entire intubation process easier to handle. Why, then, is my left hand closing into a fist? I'm not in control of its movement. It's just closing on its own and I can't open it back up.

The anesthesiologist notices this and asks if I'm OK. Oh sure, I'm fine. I'm just freaking out over here! Do something! But he doesn't. He lets me breathe into the mask a little longer as if nothing strange is happening. I can tell by the look on his face that he's worried.

I don't know if I can go through with the operation anymore. I don't feel comfortable here. I want to go back to my children's hospital where the staff knows how to treat the idiosyncrasies connected to rare syndromes like mine. But it's too late to back out now. Before I know it, I'm saying goodbye to my mom, and the nurses are whisking me back to the operating room. I don't know if it's the medicine someone administered to calm me down or if it's the nerves themselves, but I fall asleep before I'm even moved onto the operating table.

I wake up hours later in the recovery room. I open my eyes and I can see everything. Why? My eyes are usually swollen shut. I had dermal tissue grafts from my hip placed into my cheeks and chin. I feel tight and swollen everywhere in my face, but I can see. Wow! This is amazing.

Before I know it, my mom enters the room with my hearing aid. I'm sitting up in the bed, and I wave at her as she walks over to my bedside. She's can't believe how spirited and awake I appear. Truthfully, neither can I. This is unbelievable.

I'm doing so well in the recovery area that Dr. Wolfe moves me into a single room for the night. This was supposed to be an outpatient procedure, but it's getting late. For the first time, I don't mind staying overnight. I can see everything going on around me, and it's comforting.

My mom spends the night, too, and we stay up for hours watching movies on television. I'm not really tired, but I know I should rest, so eventually I start to doze.

* * *

OCTOBER 29, 2005

Dr. Wolfe stops by in the morning to see me. He yanks out the drainage tubes from the incisions under my eyes and tells me I'm being discharged soon. It all happens so fast, I can't tell if it hurts at all or if it just startles me.

Another surgery has come and gone. It's amazing that it's already over. I was terrified of this new hospital at first, but it really wasn't a horrible experience. I have to remember that everything I choose to do is a step closer to erasing the characteristics of my syndrome. Not that I'm ashamed of it. I just want to blend in with everyone else. I really think the work I had in this procedure will bring me one step closer to the confidence I seek.

More Than Physically Scarred

I know I don't do very well expressing when I'm sad or hurt. I never want to focus on those emotions, but they definitely do have a hold on me. I'm reminded every day about the hardships I face. I look into the mirror each morning as I prepare for work and I stare directly into my reflection. I don't recognize the woman staring back at me. She is not the me I see in my dreams. She is not the perfect combination of her mother and father. She is scarred and damaged.

The scars under my eyes become the focal points of my gaze. These scars are the remnants of multiple surgeries to correct the drooping of my lower eyelids. The need to correct one flaw resulted in another. When I get dressed, I run my fingers over the twelve-inch scar near my right hip where Dr. Wolfe removed bone and cartilage to use for my facial reconstruction. As I brush my hair and throw it up in a bun, I first part it at the bald spot stretched across my skull like a headband. This is the area where the surgeon sliced my head and pulled down the skin to access the bone structure underneath when he performed craniotomies. Surgery after surgery this occurred. The hair stopped growing back, and I have a permanent part bisecting the front and back of my head.

Despite all my imperfections, I'm more than just visibly scarred. The unique details I notice every morning hint at deeper stories. When I look in the mirror, I don't see only those physical imperfections; I sense the emotional scarring also left behind. These scars are the more difficult ones for me to deal with. They're the ones no one else sees. Though I don't show it, sometimes the emotional scars affect me more than the physical. They are ever present.

Each surgery stole a part of my innocence, ate away at my love of life, and left traces of misery in its wake. Often it was more than just misery; it was absolute terror. Sometimes I close my eyes and I can see it all so clearly: the moment the breathing tube was ripped from my throat when my doctor wanted to wean me off a respirator, and I was left gasping for breath; and the time I woke up paralyzed in intensive care, the result of a certain medication I was given so I wouldn't move (which no one bothered to tell me about prior to the surgery). I've voiced these memories to only a few people over the years. What was the point of telling everyone? They probably wouldn't care. They certainly wouldn't be able to relate.

The lasting impressions my medical procedures have left on me began the moment I entered this world. My parents told me that right after I was born, I was the subject of multiple tests and examinations. In each instance, I had to be strapped down onto an examination table so I would remain immobile. The doctors kept me lying on my back until they completed their analyses. I must have hated this. I must have been in a lot of pain as I lay on my back, fully restrained, while the doctors probed and jabbed at me. I must have felt trapped.

Once my parents brought me home from the hospital, they noticed that when they laid me down on my back, I would scream violently. But when they placed me on my stomach, I became quiet. It was the only way I would fall sleep. Even a car ride was a difficult task; the reclining car seat must have simulated the feeling of lying on my back. In panic, I would scream and wail until we reached our destination. My parents dreaded car rides with me, knowing I would scream the entire time.

Upon returning home after each of my surgeries, I would always sleep with my mom, no matter how old I was. She made sure I stayed off my face, which had just been surgically treated, and that I slept on my back. In the hospital, my sleep was not an issue because I had an inclined bed that forced me to stay in one position. At home, though, in my own bed, I tried everything in my power to roll onto my side. My mom always caught me mid-roll and forced me onto my back. Even now, more than thirty years later, I lie face up only when absolutely necessary.

I encountered at least one negative moment during each of my surgeries. As my collection of terrible memories grew, so did my fear of enduring more operations. I knew I had to keep moving forward, though, despite the anxiety each nightmarish moment caused. Sometimes that was hard to do. If I watched medical shows late at night, I'd often dream that I was the one going under the knife. In my dreams, I watched the anesthesiologist and nurses buzz around me as they covered my mouth with the mask. The bright overhead lights drowned out their features. The more breaths I took, the hazier everything became. I somehow forced myself to wake up from these nightmares, but they seemed so much like the reality I knew. Sometimes it was hard to decipher what was real and what my brain conjured up. I worked to calm myself down once I realized I was not in an operating room. This was my bed, my room.

By the same token, I always dreamt about my operations a few days before my scheduled procedures. Those fear-induced visions were extremely accurate, with one difference: I didn't feel any pain. In those dreams, I went through the entire process. I registered, waited anxiously in the pre-operation area, underwent the anesthesia, and then woke up in the recovery room. I was aware of my trepidations in the dreams; I was afraid of the pain I might feel and wondered what condition I would be in after the operation.

In my dreams, when I woke up in the recovery room, I would tell myself, "See, Kristin? It wasn't that bad, and now it's all over! You were afraid for no reason." No sooner than I thought that, however, I would wake up and realize the surgery hadn't happened yet. And knowing everything I did about my prior surgeries, I would lie in bed fearful about what was ahead of me, reliving all the negative moments of the past.

My parents always thought the most harrowing surgery I endured was the one to reposition my mandible and maxilla bones. It was easy to see why. That surgery required the most work, longest hospital stay, and most recovery time. It didn't, however, leave me with too much emotional damage.

It was the simple surgery, in 1999, to insert a metal device into my jaw that caused me the greatest turmoil. The surgery itself was a breeze, but the months that followed left me reeling in pain. I suffered the most agonizing torture, and I'll never be rid of that memory.

The day after my discharge from the hospital, I waited in Dr. Wolfe's office to be called in for the next phase of the jaw distraction procedure. Up to that point, I had not had any distraction procedures performed on me because I was still healing from the surgery. Today, however, would be the first time the distractor would be adjusted—the first time my jaw would be forcibly separated while I was awake.

I didn't really comprehend the severity of the situation. Either I didn't think it through beforehand, or I pushed it out of my mind completely. Whatever the case, I did not realize at that moment that somehow this device was going to lengthen my jaw by essentially ripping it apart.

The nurse called my name and led me to the room that was commonly used for in-office procedures. It was larger than most examination rooms and had a wall lined with surgical equipment. In the middle of the room was an examination table, not simply a chair, as appeared in the other rooms. Above the table hung a medical light, a type of surgical lamp commonly used to spotlight an area of the face or body. I thought nothing of it at the time, but now that room is synonymous with unimaginable pain.

I took a seat on the exam table and waited for the doctor to appear. As he entered the room, I still thought he was going to look me over and tell me to come back in a few weeks. He didn't. He told me to lie back, and he took a seat in a chair next to the table. "I'll do the first one to show you how this is done," he told my mom. Show her how *what* is done? What was he doing? These metal spokes protruding from my skin were not just decoration; they served a purpose. Dr. Wolfe held up something that resembled a screwdriver and placed it over the end of one of the spokes. He instructed my mom that each spoke should be turned one full rotation.

I didn't take me long to realize the agony behind a single turn of the spoke. With each rotation, the device pushed the jawbone outward ever so slightly. Even though the jaw only moved about 0.5 mm with each full turn, the pain was unbearable. My eyes widened and I clutched the sides of the table to alleviate the pain, the only comfort I could think of.

Dr. Wolfe had performed this act multiple times in the past, so he was very skilled in his approach. He was used to feeling the resistance of the bone against the device, and knew precisely how much torque to exert upon the screwdriver. It wasn't quite as simple as winding a music box, but he had a proper feel for what needed to be done. In a few moments, he had completed the full rotation of the first spoke. What a relief, I thought to myself. But now it was time for the other one. Dr. Wolfe advised my mother that she would perform this one, as she needed to become comfortable with the process.

My mom took hold of the screwdriver and readied herself. I could tell she was nervous, not wanting to be the bearer of pain. Nor did I want my jaw being forced apart. But what choice did either one of us have? She turned the spoke slowly and the torture started again. This was one of those Band-Aid situations—she had to learn how to turn it faster so the pain would be over sooner. I wanted to kick and scream and stop the cruelty. Bone was not meant to be forced apart like this!

Though the whole ordeal lasted less than a minute, it was the longest minute of my life. The worst part, though, was that I was told I would have to endure this torture every day, twice a day. I wasn't sure I could handle that. But Dr. Wolfe told me I had no choice in the matter. So every morning and every evening, I assumed my position while one of my parents stood over me and administered what I could describe only as medieval torture.

I felt less human having metal protruding from my skin. I was more aware of children staring at me than ever before. This metal made me a machine, not a sixteen-year-old high school student. Even though everyone noticed the metal spokes, they could never understand their purpose. No one ever asked, and I never told. They were better off not knowing; otherwise I'd have to explain the whole gruesome procedure to them.

During the time this device was attached to my jaw, my mouth remained wired shut. Instead of using wire, though, the orthodontist preferred thick rubber bands attached to my braces. Both served the same purpose. They kept my jaw stable and allowed the bone to grow, filling in the gap created by the rotations. Had he chosen to use wire, I would have been on a completely liquid diet until the distractor was removed. However, because the orthodontist chose to use rubber bands, I could remove them to eat one meal of pureed food per day.

After one week, I just wanted a hamburger. I usually had my meal at dinner, and my mom did the best she could to satisfy my cravings for real food. She pureed sirloin in place of burgers. She mashed potatoes and carrots. She made me smoothies every morning, and if I wanted ice cream, I could have it any time of the day. But eating every meal from a food processor took its toll. The teenage girls at school commented on how lucky I was to be so skinny. I stood five feet, three inches and weighed ninety-eight pounds. I told them they were the lucky ones for being able to eat real food whenever they wanted. More importantly, they were the lucky ones for being ignorant to my situation and the pain I felt every day.

The effects of this procedure stayed with me long after the doctors removed the distractor. I now compare all pain I experience to the feeling of my jawbone being forcefully expanded. That is the benchmark for pain, as far as I am concerned. I doubt anything will ever surpass it.

I saw a documentary about Treacher Collins syndrome years ago, which followed one young boy who had the same device surgically implanted. At one point, the father told him it was time to turn his spokes, and paralyzing fear washed over his face. That was my reaction, too, when I heard the father say that. It's as if that boy's life was my life being played out on television. I felt his fear as surely as he did.

My jaw surgery will always represent more than just a bad memory. It will be a tear in my soul, a personal devastation that can never be mended or healed. No matter how tough I think I am, that incident always finds a way to bring me to my knees.

The emotional scars from all my surgeries made me wonder why I should undergo more operations. The older I grew, the more vividly I could remember the hardship and pain each procedure caused me. I knew those feelings would not dissipate over time. But I always felt there was more to be done, so I had to press on. I also knew I could not stop until I truly felt I had done enough.

I had my last surgery in 2010, and after that I vowed never to go under the knife again if it wasn't absolutely necessary. This was my third surgery at South Miami Hospital, and each time the anesthesiologist there struggled with my narrow airway. Even though the hospital had been advised ahead of time that I required intubation with a fiber optic scope, preparations were not made in advance to have such a device available. As I lay in the pre-op hospital bed trying to calm my nerves with deep yoga breathing, the anesthesiologist assigned to my procedure introduced himself. My mom once again mentioned my tight airway, but he didn't seem concerned. He told me I would be in a twilight sleep for the intubation, but assured me I would not remember a thing. I hoped he was right.

After all my previous surgeries, I never knew I was technically awake when they inserted the breathing tube down my throat. The combination of drugs they used to induce this twilight state left me sedated yet responsive. It would also cause temporary memory loss, which could explain why I never knew I had been awake.

Even though I trusted what the doctor told me, my nerves skyrocketed. I had a feeling this surgery was going to be a memorable one, but for all the wrong reasons. I was right.

Once the entire team was ready, they wheeled me into the operating room and administered the drugs to knock me out. I knew the ritual. Ten-nine-eight . . . and then I was out. But something unusual happened during this procedure. I never seemed to lose consciousness. I remember staring up at five people hovering over my body trying to shove a tube down my throat.

"OK, Kristin. Breathe. Don't struggle," someone said. I choked on the tube, gagged, and coughed as they tried to snake it down my airway. I wasn't supposed to be awake! Why was I awake? The awareness didn't last, but the moment etched itself in my mind forever. I can still see the anesthesiology team standing above me. I can hear them. I can feel my body rejecting the tube. I can sense the fear that I would stay conscious like this for the entire surgery.

I woke up in the recovery room a few hours later wondering how I would ever be able to face that again. The panic I experienced when I saw all those people struggling to intubate me was indescribable. I never want to go through anything like that again. So I won't. Not unless I absolutely have to. My days of elective surgeries are over. I have done enough to sculpt my face into something that makes me happy. I am all that I am going to be.

I may not often express when I'm dealing with pain or sorrow, but I feel it every day of my life. I try to drown out the memories, but they play out repeatedly in my mind. I can't escape the wounds; they're cut too deeply to ever fully heal. But these scars, as damaging as they are, make up my story. I hope they are but a very small part of it.

FEBRUARY 7, 2006

One of the reasons I decided to take a year off between my college graduation and entering the working world was so I could undergo a cornea transplant in my right eye. My vision kept worsening over the years and the keratoconus caused my cornea to grow too steep. I wore my hard contact lens when I could, but I hated it. The lens irritated my eye whenever I wore it, and I dreaded the pain it caused. I began to wear my contact less and less until one day it no longer fit. The slope of the eye had grown too steep for the glass to bend, preventing the contact lens from adhering to my cornea, and contacts were no longer a solution to my vision problem. If I wanted to see clearly again, I needed a cornea transplant.

Here I am at the outpatient facility waiting for my transplant to begin. This is my first surgery completely unrelated to my Treacher Collins syndrome, so I have no idea what to expect. I scheduled the surgery even before having a donor, which fascinated me. My ophthalmologist assured me he would have a donor organ at the time of my procedure. He was correct. I received word from the doctor's office shortly before the day of the operation that my cornea would come from a recently deceased fifty-seven-year-old female.

From the time I scheduled this appointment until I signed in at the outpatient facility this morning, the thought of having this surgery didn't frighten me. Now, however, as I sit in the pre-op area, I'm nervous. This is a complete unknown for me. It doesn't require my face being cut open in any way. There won't be blood, bruising, or swelling. I'll be able to see (out of one eye) and hear as soon as the doctor completes the transplant procedure. I'll even be awake through this process, though in a twilight state. Some people who have this operation are entirely conscious during the procedure and are fully aware of everything going on around them even though they are sedated with proper medication; however, that's pretty unlikely to happen to me. I shouldn't remember a single thing. And because I won't truly be asleep, I don't need to be intubated. This procedure seems so much simpler than my normal operations, yet my stomach is still anxiously churning as I wait for the doctor to bring me back into the operating room. A surgery is a surgery. The nerves will never stop.

When the nurse enters the room to insert my IV, I begin to panic. I ask her if she has anything to numb the area before inserting the IV needle. To my relief, she does. That means the worst part of this whole pre-op process is painless.

A few minutes have passed since the nurse inserted the IV, and it's now time to inject the sedative to help me drift into that twilight sleep. The nurse administers the medication and I begin to fall into a relaxed state. Finally, the world around me fades out of focus.

Suddenly I'm awake. Why am I awake? I can see my ophthalmologist looking at me intently, working on my eye. Thank God my eye is numb! He's holding a needle in his hand and it's moving closer to my cornea. This is surreal. I'm watching my own transplant happen.

Ouch! Why did I feel that prick in my eye? I'm not supposed to feel anything. I must have muttered "ouch" aloud without realizing it, because someone just injected another shot of a numbing agent into my eye. I can see my doctor threading the stitches in the cornea, but I can no longer feel the needle. What a relief. It's bad enough I'm watching the end of this procedure. I'd rather not feel it, too.

I'm now being wheeled into the post-op area. I don't actually remember the end of the surgery or how I ended up in this chair. My transplant is complete, and that's all that matters. I'm wearing an eye patch over my right eye and a plastic eye protector covering the patch. I'm told the plastic protector will prevent anything from touching the donor cornea and causing irritation. The more steps I take now to protect my cornea, the better chance I have that my body will accept it.

It's such a strange feeling for me to fully interact with others after a surgery. I'm sitting in a chair, drinking some juice, and talking with the nurses. It's hard to me to fathom that it's all really happening. As soon as the staff is confident I'm feeling well, they'll let me go home. Even though I watched the end of my transplant in action and felt the sensation of the doctor sewing the donor cornea to my eye, this entire procedure was a lot easier to bear than my craniofacial reconstruction operations.

* * *

FEBRUARY 8, 2006

I'm learning that the cornea transplant procedure itself is much simpler than the post-operative care. Today is my first of many visits to the eye doctor to monitor the progress of my body accepting the donor cornea. I will need to return to the doctor's office every few days for the first two to three weeks until my ophthalmologist is certain the new cornea is healing properly. After that, it's once every couple of weeks, and then once a month.

The doctor removes the eye patch, and I try to focus on the eye chart. My vision is still quite blurry, which will be the case for a few days. In some cases, it can take months for the donor cornea to fully bond with the eyeball, and vision might not reach its clearest state until that happens. It's been only a day, but so far everything looks normal. The doctor removes the protective lens that was covering the cornea, and I immediately wish he would put it back on. I didn't even realize I was wearing anything over my cornea, but as soon as he removed it, I could feel the sutures scratching my inner eyelid as I opened and closed my eye. The lens protector prevented this scratching, but he couldn't leave it in too long. He said I just had to get used to the feeling.

* * *

FEBRUARY 15, 2006

I'm healing nicely. I continue to sleep with the plastic eye protector covering my right eye so I don't roll over onto my face and damage the cornea. I have a tendency to roll over, so this shield is a life-saver. I'm lucky I don't have a job during this healing time and I can spend as much time as I need recuperating. I have had a very difficult time adjusting to light since the transplant. This is normal, but it's an arduous process nonetheless. I spend most of my days on the couch watching television; however, I can't keep my eyes open for very long because the brightness of the room is physi-cally painful. I try to focus on the television set, but I have to fight to keep my eyes open for as long as possible until I can't tolerate the brightness any longer. My sensitivity to light will decrease over time as the transplant site heals. Until then, I'll lie on the couch wondering just how people go about their normal lives after this surgery when I can barely stand to keep my eyes open.

AUGUST 13, 2006

While I was at work yesterday, I felt a small pop in my right eye. I thought I'd imagined it, but soon after, I experienced excruciating pain in my eye. It felt like tiny shards of glass each time I opened and closed my eyelid. I could tell something wasn't right. In my six months of recovery, the transplant had never caused this much pain. Sure, the stitches irritated my inner eyelid for a month or so after the transplant until I built up a tolerance for the scratching, but it was always an uncomfortable feeling, not painful.

I begged my manager to let me leave work early because I needed to drive down to Boca Raton for an emergency eye doctor appointment. My parents drove the three hours to Orlando to pick me up and we immediately turned the car around and headed back down to South Florida. There was no way I could have made that three-hour drive myself. I was in so much pain that I could barely keep my eye open. I wasn't sure I would make it through the night being in so much pain, but I had to do the best I could.

The eye doctor's office opened especially for me today. It's Sunday, but luckily a cornea specialist is able to take my emergency case. We are all worried what might have happened. What had caused so much pain? Did I do something wrong? The doctor looks at my right eye through an optical magnifying lens and immediately notices the problem. A suture has come undone. The little pop I felt was the stitch breaking apart, and the extreme pain I felt was the exposed tip of the suture jabbing me in the eye.

The doctor easily removes the broken stitch with a pair of tweezers, and the discomfort fades away. He tells us this might continue to happen. In some patients, the stitches remain intact forever, but for others like myself, they break. He can't remove the stitches prematurely, because that could cause damage to the cornea. There's no telling if or when more sutures will rupture, but if they do, I will now know the feeling. We are all in agreement that I should find an eye doctor in Orlando, where I now live, in case this happens again.

My vision is still stable despite this setback. My doctor is pleased with the progress of my healing and will continue to monitor my condition. I can't explain how unbelievable it is to read the eye chart out of my right eye. My vision used to be 20/200, but now it's 20/50, with the chance to continue improving. This transplant has had a tremendous impact on my life. I drive at night a little more easily, I judge depth a little better, and I use both eyes to look at my surroundings. I feel like I can see the world again.

I'd love to tell you I'm 100 percent accepting of who I am these days, but I'm not. I've grown hypersensitive to the way people look at me. I can't shake the feeling that I'm being judged on my appearance with a single glance or a moment of hesitation. Does the manager at the coffee shop keep walking past the counter because he's looking at my face? Is the cashier at the drive-thru speaking slowly to me because she doesn't think I can understand her? I wonder if that group of teenagers is making fun of me. They didn't start laughing until I walked by them.

I'm sure most of the time my vulnerable self reacts to these situations before my brain has a moment to analyze them. The manager probably wants to take note of the growing line. The cashier probably wants to make sure she is handing me the correct order and change. The kids are no doubt laughing about a joke they just heard. I'm not the cause. I'm not even a blip on their radar. Nevertheless, the nagging voice in the back of my mind says the world is gawking at me because of my unique appearance.

I wasn't always this way, but over time, self-doubt crept into my life and suffocated the confidence my parents worked so hard to instill in me. The older I became, the more I realized I wasn't an ordinary kid like my family led me to believe. I grew more aware of my issues with each passing year and each painful procedure. What others think of my appearance no longer should affect me after all these years, after all these operations, but it does. I'd love to be free of these feelings of inadequacy; however, I've spent my life being scrutinized by the eyes of a skilled artist, my doctor. With each imperfection Dr. Wolfe corrected, he found a new one to improve on.

I used to wonder why a person would willingly undergo plastic surgery to transform a face that, in my opinion, was already ideal. There was so much beauty in the world that people looked to alter, to improve. I used to believe I would never willingly choose to undergo surgeries if I didn't have a facial deformity. But as I grew older, I began to understand. I developed the habit of spotting the flaws too. I sought out my visible imperfections and amplified them. I brought them into focus and kept them in the center of my thoughts until I changed them with Dr. Wolfe's help. Even after I changed them, I always found more. I created a negative voice in my head telling me that my reflection needed to be improved. There was no way I would ever completely be free from my syndrome, yet still I sought unattainable perfection.

I continue to pinpoint these imperfections even today. Some are so minor that only I notice them. When I smile, one eye opens more than the other. I detect that unevenness in photos all the time. There's a dimple on my right cheek below my eye and a depression underneath that cheek that I would love to fill. My top lip is extremely thin, which is why I never wear lipstick to draw attention to the area. In the mirror, my eyes zoom in on the unevenness of my eyebrows, the asymmetry of my jaw, and the barely noticeable depression on the tip of my nose. I see these flaws, and I constantly compare myself to others without a syndrome, though I know I shouldn't; I know that's not healthy. But these imperfections are my own. As often as I wish I could change every little blemish, I understand that will never happen. I think I'll always notice the little details that others might not, but I have to realize that those details make me uniquely Kristin. I know I'll never be free of these thoughts, though.

My confidence takes a giant leap backward when I bump into someone I haven't seen since childhood and they comment on how I look the same now as I did back then. I don't. Please do not tell me otherwise. My appearance has been altered so much over the years. I do not look the same at thirty-three as I did at three years old, or sixteen years old, or even twenty-two years old. I'm proud of my sculpted cheeks and constructed jaw. Each reconstructive procedure added another layer of hope to my life. By telling me my looks haven't changed, people devalue each one of those painful surgeries that was meant to diminish the effects of my syndrome.

My friends reassure me that they no longer notice the Treacher Collins traits. They tell me I'm beautiful the way I am, but that's hard for me to accept. *Beautiful* is a word I have a difficult time correlating with my physical appearance. Growing up, I never thought of myself as ugly, but I certainly wasn't beautiful. I just felt awkward. No one else I knew walked around with metal protruding from their body or had stubs for ears. I felt like I was in a league of my own and couldn't—or shouldn't—be compared to anyone else. To me, personal beauty meant eliminating all signs of my facial anomaly, something I knew would never happen, yet I worked toward that goal with each reconstructive surgery.

I've come a long way from the baby who was born in 1982. Even after all this time, I'm still growing into myself; I'm still adjusting to the features that have been developed throughout the years. It's hard for me to accept when someone considers me attractive, because I still feel like I am that gawky, awkward pre-teen. I know I'm not. I'm so much more than awkward, but when someone calls me beautiful, I assume they're just being polite.

My opinion of myself has changed over the years. I understand I'm attractive in my own way. I still bear the scars and symptoms of my syndrome, but I'm much more confident now than I used to be. I walk taller and smile bigger than I did before all of my surgeries. But even though I can see the beauty in my appearance, I still have a hard time believing anyone else who says it. I battle with this feeling of self-doubt every day.

My personal insecurities aren't the sole cause of my struggles with self-acceptance. How random strangers view my syndrome greatly affects how I view myself. Some people consider Treacher Collins to be "special needs," while other, less tolerant people, consider it an abomination, or, even worse, an act of the devil. I found each of these opinions on the Internet. They exist. Though these comments weren't made directly toward me, I felt the sting of the words as I read them. I'm still a representative of Treacher Collins syndrome. Those comments were meant for someone just like me. I am neither special needs nor an abomination; none of us with Treacher Collins is. We are able-bodied human beings who have our own unique struggles. My abnormal facial structure required surgeries, but they did not limit my abilities. Treacher Collins syndrome did not make me any less human.

My story might be unique to me, but my struggle with confidence is universal. We live in a society in which the quest for perfection works on overdrive. Beauty is subjective, but everywhere I look I'm told how to rid myself of imperfections that other people call out as flaws. Our culture promotes unblemished skin, chiseled features, and thin figures. I'm forced to compare myself to a minuscule percent of the population that fits that mold. How can I have confidence if I know I'll never reach these ideals? How can anyone?

When I was about thirteen, a relative took me for my first makeover. I felt so amazing sitting on the stool as the makeup artist applied every product imaginable. My face was caked in foundation and powder, a sensation I couldn't get used to. I thought for sure my scars would be hidden under all that goop. She brushed the blush over my cheeks, and I sensed the chiseled appearance of cheekbones forming. She swiped eye shadow on my lids, outlined my eyes, and lengthened my lashes with mascara. Surely, I thought, my eyes were going to be formed into more symmetrical, oval shapes after all this makeup. Lastly, she applied a bright-red liner and then lipstick. I hoped this would plump up my top lip!

After the artist applied all of the makeup, she held a mirror in front me. I was so eager to see my reflection. I must look like a rock star wearing all this makeup, I thought. But as she flipped the mirror around to face me, I stared back into the reflection of a clown. My appearance hadn't improved; it had actually worsened with the various layers of product. The bright lipstick highlighted my thin upper lip; it didn't subdue it. My eyelids appeared even heavier with the dark eye shadow, and the eye liner only emphasized the odd shape of my eyes. The sloppily applied pink blush drew attention to my underdeveloped cheekbones. I wanted to jump off that chair and run home as quickly as I could. I was so embarrassed. Despite everything in my life, I had never before been ashamed of my appearance—not until looking at my reflection that day. I know I shouldn't have thought makeup would diminish the traits of my syndrome, but because it helped emphasize everyone else's attractiveness, I thought it would improve mine.

I was only thirteen, a teenager. I still had a long road of reconstruction ahead of me with the most impactful procedures in the near future. At that age, I was confident in myself as a person, but not in my looks. I would one day learn that the less-is-more approach to makeup works best for me, but at the time, I felt so betrayed by these products that were supposed to improve my appearance. They did nothing but draw attention to the very features I hoped to hide. If I continued to compare myself to everyone I knew, all the actresses I saw on television, and the models in the magazines, I would never learn to appreciate my own beauty.

These days, I've given up trying to reach the high standards set by society. Many days I throw my hair up in a ponytail, clip my bangs back, and don't put on makeup. I expose my hearing aid and misshapen ears. I don't cover up the redness underneath my lower eyelids. I wear yoga pants and flip-flops. I'm not trying to impress anyone. I'm just showing the world the real me, the girl who is scarred and different. I know I'll never live up to my culture's definition of perfection. Very few people will. I'm OK with that. But to some extent, my quest for perfection probably always will be there, whether I like it or not.

The emphasis on flawlessness isn't new. Throughout history, people with deformities were cast aside as unsuitable to society. People like myself were left for dead at birth, accused of being cursed, or ruthlessly killed, all because our abnormal appearances instilled fear in people. Instead of celebrating our uniqueness, they wanted to eliminate it.

In ancient times, the Spartans killed any newborn baby that exhibited the slightest imperfection. They did not tolerate flaws in their quest for the perfect race, and the only way to ensure the flawed didn't one day overrun the population was to immediately kill off flawed offspring. Death was our punishment in the past, and in some societies, it still is an unfortunate reality for people born different.

Nazi Germany is the perfect example of how people with disfiguring diseases faced unspeakable horrors at the hands of sadists. When I first learned about the Holocaust in grade school, I realized I would have been targeted for my facial deformity. My superior physical abilities and intelligence would not have saved me. I would have been sentenced to a merciless death along with millions of other innocent victims. Prior to that death, though, I probably would have been imprisoned by some madman like Josef Mengele, the chief doctor at Auschwitz, also known as the "Angel of Death," who viewed children with disabilities as experimental subjects rather than as human beings. I no doubt would have been forced to endure countless torturous experiments all in the name of twisted science.

My innocence was shaken simply by learning about these horrible acts. Fear, anger, and sadness ate away at my comfort. Had I lived in another time, I would have been subjected to cruelty solely because of my appearance. I wondered whether history might someday repeat itself and I might be targeted for my facial abnormality. Bizarre thoughts entered my mind. I felt burdened and vulnerable just thinking about what happened to others before me—and what might have happened to me if lived in another era.

Since then, I have never been able to forget that there are people in this world who will always see me as a person with a deformity before they see me as a human being. Knowing not everyone embraces differences is perhaps the most hurtful and frightening realization I will ever make. It's one of the reasons I will never be free from all insecurity.

I choose to see all people as human beings; I don't dwell on whether someone's skin is a different color, what religion he might be, or whether he has a disability. My parents instilled in me the importance of acceptance and kindness. If I expected people to treat me with openness and love, I needed to act the same way toward others. Because of my family, I learned never to judge others and to accept all people as they are. I'm a lot less critical of other people than I am of myself. I never notice their flaws, though mine never leave my thoughts.

Despite everything, I do love the person I've become. My traces of Treacher Collins have diminished with each operation. I'm proud of the changes. I'm proud that after everything I've been through, I can still walk through life with a smile on my face. Yes, it has been rough, but my surgeries helped improve my self-confidence, even if they did also cause me to be more critical of my imperfections. I'll no doubt continue to find faults, and my insecurities will never disappear completely. But each day I'm learning to grow more and more comfortable in my own skin. It's a continuous learning process and an obvious challenge, but one of these days I will fully embrace the effects of my syndrome.

And even if I do struggle to accept all of my imperfections, I will never quit showing the world the beauty that someone with a facial abnormality can possess.

JULY 10, 2007

Now that I'm older, most of my reconstructive operations will be
elective. Each surgery still helps minimize the noticeable traits of
Treacher Collins, but they're more like minor tweaks than full-
blown reconstruction. Today's procedure is very much elective and
should be quite simple. Dr. Wolfe is taking a few layers of skin from
my clavicles and placing them underneath my lower eyes to cover
up the scarring from the many previous surgeries. This process
is known as full-thickness skin grafts. The skin on the clavicles
closely resembles the facial skin. It has the same texture and color-
ation, meaning it will blend in well with the skin on my face.

I admit that this procedure probably isn't a necessity, but I'm
only twenty-four years old and I worry about my appearance. At
times, I can be vain. The scarring and wrinkly skin under my eyes
truly bothers me, so when Dr. Wolfe recommended this procedure, I willingly accepted.

* * *

JULY 11, 2007

Yesterday as I was recovering from my surgery, I felt the effects of
the anesthesia more than any other time I can remember. When a
nurse came into the hospital room to check my vital signs, a wave
of nausea hit me hard. I wanted to tell the nurse to move out of the
way, but the only thing that came out of my mouth was vomit. He
came in to see how I was feeling, and I threw up all over his shoes.
How embarrassing.

* * *

JULY 16, 2007

I look like a football player. The new skin grafts have turned a deep eggplant color, making it look like I've applied rectangles of black grease under my eyes. Dr. Wolfe tells me this is normal. The top two layers of skin die and crust off, but the bottom layers take. I'll continue to keep the area protected and covered with gauze until it heals entirely. I'll come back for another post-op checkup next week. It's a waiting game now.

* * *

AUGUST 13, 2007

It took an entire month for the skin grafts to take! It usually happens much faster, and I know Dr. Wolfe was worried my body might reject the grafts in the end. In that case, we would have had to start from scratch. I'm grateful everything worked out. Even though this procedure was relatively easy, I'm not ready to go under the knife again any time soon. In fact, I think I might be finished with surgeries altogether. I can't think of what else might need to be corrected.

This was supposed to be the chapter about my dating life, but this is the one area of my life in which I haven't been able to create even the slightest semblance of normalcy. I'm thirty-three years old and I've never been on a date, never been kissed, and never had a boyfriend. That's one of the hardest facts about my life that I have had to admit. It's probably even more difficult than the haunting memories of all my surgeries. Those nightmares are moments in the past. This is my reality, my present, and quite possibly my future.

My insecurities led me to believe that I somehow wasn't worth dating because of my syndrome. In high school, I had my jaw distraction surgery, which left me very self-aware due to the exposed metal device. My confidence was shaken, and I figured no one would want to date a girl who continually underwent such abnormal medical procedures. Since then, during every operation, I reassured myself that it was better to be alone during these personal struggles. I had my family by my side to help me through and heal. I didn't think many other people would be able to handle seeing me suffer through these extensive ordeals that left me battered and broken. And because there would always be more procedures in my future, it would never be the right time for a boyfriend. My operations became the scapegoat for my lack of a dating life.

Still, with every year that passed, I wondered when I would get a chance to participate in the dating game. Surely I had to meet someone willing to accept my imperfections in college if it didn't happen in high school, right? If not in college, then by my mid-twenties? In my thirties? I've passed thirty, and I'm still not sure when or if I'll experience all of the "firsts" associated with dating. I feel like such a loser. I feel like I'm being left behind while all of my friends marry, have families, and move on with their lives. My life is frustratingly stagnant. They're moving on, and I'm still here . . . alone. I've never had the chance to love or to fall in love. I've never had the opportunity to mend a broken heart. I've never had much to add to a conversation about dating. My experience is practically nonexistent.

This setback is entirely my fault, not my syndrome's. I lack self-esteem, I'm shy, and I'm picky. I could never find a good enough reason why someone would choose to date me instead of a girl without so many visible problems. Even though I'm funny, adventurous, and a hard-core baseball fan, it's almost as if I don't think I'm worthy of being loved, as if I think I have nothing to offer. Instead of emphasizing all of my positive qualities, I focus solely on my syndrome. This is my downfall. I have only myself to blame.

All the years I spent trying to convince myself it wasn't the right time to have a boyfriend because of my surgeries, it was all just an excuse. I placed blame where it didn't belong. In reality, I never took the initiative. The only times I ever slow-danced with boys at school dances were the times when my friends told the boys to ask me. While I appreciated their efforts, it felt so awkward dancing with someone I thought would have rather spent that song with another girl. I didn't want to be a charity case.

When something excited me enough to put myself out there, it backfired. In sixth grade, we took a field trip to Kennedy Space Center in Cape Canaveral, Florida. On the bus ride home, a group of my friends played truth or dare. I always hated the unknown of that game and how it put me on the spot, but I was feeling pretty gutsy that day. I decided to play. On my turn, someone dared me to kiss one of the popular boys. Both anxiety and excitement overcame me. I had a major crush on this boy, so I was happy he was my target. I walked over to where he sat in the back of the bus, leaned over, and puckered my lips. Just as I moved in to kiss him, he turned his head and my lips made contact with his ear. It wasn't a quiet kiss either. My lips made a loud smacking sound that I'm sure reverberated through his ears. I scurried back to my seat and tried to fade into nothingness. I felt so ashamed by what I'd done. Why did I ever think kissing the popular boy would work in my favor? I wanted to drop out of school right then and there.

That incident shouldn't have scarred me. I was young and foolish, and I'm sure plenty of people have embarrassing stories similar to mine. But I can't forget it. It haunts me because I have never had the chance to prove to myself that I am no longer that awkward pre-teen. I'm basing everything I know about kissing on a lousy, inconsequential game I played in sixth grade.

My lack of experience tends to make me think less of myself; therefore, I sometimes come off as shy and standoffish. Growing up, I always felt as if people were judging me when they stared in my direction; because of that, I associate being the focus of someone's attention with negative feelings. However, staring is also a form of flattery. I'm accustomed to having eyes on me because of my looks, but I can't decipher when those gazes mean more than just gawking at my unique appearance. If I'm in a bar and a guy can't keep his eyes off me, I think he's staring at my syndrome, not at me as a woman. The truth is I'm uncomfortable being the sole focus of someone's attention, even if his gaze is full of adoration instead of curiosity. I don't really know how to respond.

I have had a few people over the years express interest in dating me, but they always made it seem as if they only wanted to date *someone*, not necessarily me. I happened to be single, and that was good enough for them. They didn't really like me for me. They liked me because it was convenient for them. I'm never willing to be someone's *anybody* because they are lonely, or because I am lonely. I have more pride than that. I wanted to be with someone who was drawn to me for all the right reasons: my personality, my kindness, or our commonalities.

I thought about trying my luck at online dating, where I would be able to search for possible matches using our similarities. On more than one occasion using various sites, I signed up, answered the profile questions, and waited to be notified of my matches. I waited and waited and waited, but very few people contacted me. The ones who did were creeps. Even in cyberspace, I didn't succeed. I realized that people in the online world were perhaps even more superficial than those in the real world.

Online dating starts with physical attraction above all other forms of compatibility. You upload a photo and get matched with someone who sees that photo. If they like what they see, they message you—more often than not, without viewing the profile you worked tirelessly to craft. I always chose the best photo I could, but it never seemed to work. I emphasized my likes and my strengths in my profile, but I never knew the etiquette for mentioning my syndrome. If I deliberately called out my Treacher Collins, I was not staying true to myself—a self who, aside from the reminders found in memories and mirrors, felt normal. I didn't want to dwell on the negative aspects of my life when looking for a relationship. I wanted to focus on all the ways I was ordinary. But would it be fair to a potential date if I didn't mention my hearing aid and malformed ears? He might not have noticed those in the photograph. Would I want to be blindsided like that? As it turned out, I never had to worry about whether I was being fair to a match. I never even went on a date. I left each online dating site empty-handed and wishing I had never joined in the first place.

In recent years, I can't say I've tried hard to change my relationship status. I've increasingly accepted my single status and cherished the independence it provides me. I'm responsible only for myself, and I like it that way. I don't worry about disturbing someone else when I wake up at 4:30 in the morning to go for my run; I control what's on television 100 percent of the time; and I am in no way obligated to call someone every day if I don't feel like talking. Being perpetually single has allowed me to live my life on my own terms, and as selfish as it might seem, I'm now comfortable that way.

I'm actually terrified of what will happen if I do meet someone special. Being alone is all I've ever known, and I'm afraid of what will change if I introduce another person into the mix. Because of this, I don't make an effort to date, but by now I should be much more experienced with men than I am. And not necessarily on a physical level either. I should know how to flirt and make conversation with someone I'm interested in without feeling awkward. Of course, it's also embarrassing to admit that I'm still a virgin. I grow only more self-conscious about that as I age. But if I find someone, how do I even begin to tell him that I'm thirty-three and have never had sex—or even been kissed? What will he think of me? I also worry about what will happen if I do one day experience those firsts. I'm petrified of the unknown. What if I'm a terrible kisser? What if I make a mistake? I'm not a teenager anymore; I shouldn't feel this way. I'm so terrified of experiencing these things so late in life that sometimes I wonder if it's best that I don't even try to enter a relationship.

Neither morals nor virtue have kept me on this path of celibacy. My syndrome is not to blame. Only I can claim responsibility for the life I lead. I know that others with Treacher Collins, or other physical deformities, have been able to live full lives. They've been able to date, marry, and start families. They've been able to free themselves from the emotional baggage caused by their syndrome. I envy them. I wish I could rid my mind of the self-deprecating, paralyzing thoughts that have caused me to devalue my worth. If I ever want to be in a relationship, I must fully learn to love myself before I can expect anyone else to love me. That's the ultimate goal.

NOVEMBER 16, 2010

Why am I doing this? Why am I here? I keep putting myself through the same torment year after year.

Yesterday, as I pre-registered for my operation, I realized something: I could die. This surgery is supposed to be an outpatient procedure, but with any surgery there are risks involved. I signed the waiver releasing the hospital of any faults in case of an accidental death. I signed it because I had to, but I began to wonder whether I should even proceed with the surgery. It was too late to cancel, so I showed up at South Miami Hospital bright and early as planned.

Now, I'm lying here in the pre-op bed trying to calm my nerves. My mom is sitting in the chair next to the bed holding my hand and trying her best to soothe my anxiety. This sterile environment is far too familiar. The antiseptic smell fills my nostrils each time I take a breath, and suddenly all of the negative memories of the past flood my brain. What will leave a lasting impression this time? I hope it's nothing too severe. This is supposed to be a relatively simple procedure, but I can't stop the bile from rising in my throat when I think about everything that could go wrong.

Is the surgery really necessary? I know the answer: yes. Because of my TCS, my eyelids don't shut all the way when I blink or sleep. Though each surgery over the years worked to correct this issue, this particular surgery will be the most impactful. Dr. Wolfe plans to take a couple of layers of skin from the roof of my mouth and place them inside the lower eyelids. This will add more stability to the lower eyelids and prevent them from drooping downward. By doing this, my eyes will not dry out.

I know the dry-eye feeling all too well. A few years ago, the air conditioning in my apartment broke and the repairman couldn't come to fix it until the following day. I slept with the fan running all night long, and my eyes severely dried out. When I woke up the next morning, they felt scratchy like sandpaper and I struggled to keep them open. My eye doctor prescribed a few different types of drops to use until my eyes healed, and he instructed me never to sleep with the fan on again.

So yes, I remind myself, this surgery is absolutely necessary. If I don't improve the function of my lids, my eyes will dry out too much. This can lead to ulcers or even complete loss of vision, neither of which I want.

The second part of the surgery, however, is almost fully elective. Dr. Wolfe will take fat from my thighs and inject it into my cheeks. It's another way to add volume to the cheeks and replace the soft tissue that has been absorbed over the years. The fat injections are not a necessity, but as long as I am having the eyelid surgery, I want to rebuild the tissue that has been lost. I feel like I will always be a work in progress. Whether or not I take action to continue this progress is entirely up to me now.

At the moment, I want everything to be over. I'm ready to go home. The anesthesiologist makes an appearance and tells me not to worry. I'll be in twilight sleep for the intubation, but I won't remember a thing. My mind races and I begin to freak out even more. Let's just start this operation. The sooner I'm put to sleep, the sooner I can wake up and leave.

Shortly after all the staff has visited my bedside, I'm wheeled back into surgery. I know the routine. The breathing mask is placed over my mouth, and in a few seconds, I'm out cold.

But I'm not out. I'm awake and struggling to fight the tube being forced down my throat. I'm coughing and gagging and trying to will myself to fall asleep. My awareness only lasts a few seconds, but I hear the anesthesiologist and see him standing over me. I thought he said I wouldn't remember anything. He lied, and if I see him again, I'm going to tell him he lied. I remember the entire, awful ordeal.

The next thing I know, I'm waking up in the recovery room. I can barely open my eyes, but that's nothing unusual for me. My body has become accustomed over the years to the effects of surgery, and it isn't long before my mom is able to join me with my hearing aid. I look at her out of two slivers of openings that are my eyes, and we start to talk. It turns out that I have a couple stitches in each eye holding the bottom eyelids in place. This will help the area inside the eyelids heal properly. These stitches are the reason I cannot open my eyes any wider. They'll remain in place until I visit Dr. Wolfe's office in a few days.

As I wait to be discharged, the anesthesiologist comes over to say hello. He tells my mom and me that they had some trouble intubating me and he had to call in two other anesthesiologists to help him. When I tell him I know all about that, and that I saw them all standing above me as they were trying to intubate me, he is shocked. He thought I would have no recollection of the event at all. Oh, but I do. And I'll never be able to forget it either, thank you! Right now, though, I don't want to dwell on it. I just want to go home. I'm thankful this was truly an outpatient procedure, and in a few minutes, I'll be in the car leaving this place. I hope this is the last memory I'll ever take away from this hospital, from any hospital. After twenty-seven years, I'm ready to put my syndrome behind me.

Like everyone else, I wanted to choose a career path that was both exciting and rewarding. When I was young, I thought that path would lead me to a career in medicine, the chosen field of my mother. It did not. I learned from my many hospital visits that I never wanted to work in the medical field; I didn't want the constant reminder of my own operations. My love of athletics didn't entice me to follow a career in health or nutrition either; I saw sports as more of a hobby than anything else. As for the possibility of becoming an advocate for those with disabilities, that is something I prefer to do as an avocation rather than as a career. My long-term goal is to someday organize a marathon or some other event to increase awareness of Treacher Collins syndrome and to raise money for affected families that might need help with medical expenses.

When it came time for me to enter the working world, I knew from experience that I could do whatever I wanted, I just hadn't figured out what that was yet. I didn't want to make the wrong choice, and I definitely didn't want to settle for just anything.

After graduating college with a bachelor's degree in fine arts and with far too little work experience, I decided to move to Orlando, three hours north of my hometown, where I landed a retail sales job with a large company I had always admired. It wasn't much, but I intended to stay at this job for three months at the most while I figured out my next steps in life.

Little did I know that that temporary job would lead to something much more fulfilling. Just as I had done my entire life, I worked hard and demonstrated to my employers that I was someone worth noticing. In no time, my diligence and extra effort earned the respect of my managers and peers, fast-tracking my career and allowing me to climb my way up the company ladder. Eventually I was promoted into a position in the product development department, where I help create the merchandise I once sold in stores.

Throughout all of my years with the company, I have never felt judged by my appearance. In adopting the same friendly and approachable persona I had as a child, I have shown my employer that I am no different from anyone else who works there. My opportunities have been unlimited.

Unfortunately, I can't say the same about some other career opportunities I have explored. In one instance, I applied for a position with a large retailer in California. My phone interviews went great, my job qualifications were spot on, and I thought I would get the job. My hopes were dashed, however, when I received the dreaded email: "We're sorry, but you don't have the proper math skills for the position." I was crushed, especially since math had been one of my best subjects throughout my schooling. Did the decision-maker from this company find me on social media and see that I was different? I guess I'll never know. But when one has Treacher Collins syndrome, being judged on physical appearance is always a possibility.

I don't know where I'm going next in my career or what the future holds for me in general, but I've learned to accept the unknown. I've gotten to where I am today by taking chances and proving that I deserve the opportunities I've been given. I've learned to trust my instincts, to go with the flow, and to never let my syndrome prevent me from growing. And I plan to keep growing as long as I can.

My life was defined the moment I entered the world in December 1982, and it has proven to be anything but ordinary. I was born with Treacher Collins syndrome, endured ten facial reconstructive surgeries, numerous oral surgeries, and a cornea transplant. Looking back on everything, my life has been a struggle—some might say a disaster, even—but I very rarely let my syndrome control me. I'd like to think I've handled my situation well, the best I could.

I try not to question why I received a genetic mutation. There isn't really a reason to do so; I can't change anything. Sometimes, though, I wonder what it would be like to live someone else's life, to see the world through different eyes. I wonder what my life would have been like if I had blended in with the crowds, if I had never undergone operations, or if I had dated in high school. Would I have found stability in strength or earned honors in school? Would I have understood the importance of kindness and acceptance? Would I still be the same person I am today if I hadn't dealt with such extensive problems?

There really isn't a point in dwelling on the "what ifs." This is my reality. It is the only life I will ever know. Other people with TCS have known the same challenges, some much worse. My surgeries may have left behind physical scars and emotional insecurities, but they also taught me that I could handle life's obstacles. I've struggled, but I've succeeded. This life may have had its disastrous moments, many of which will haunt me forever, but the ordinary moments in between those disasters certainly were beautiful. I have a family who loves me, friends who accept me, and memories that are irreplaceable. I've done pretty well for myself despite the hardships.

Of course, my life continues to evolve. The more I endure, the more I feel the effects of my syndrome. Over the years, every operation left me feeling even more aware of my unique situation. With each doctor's appointment and stare from a stranger, my naïveté faded and I became more self-conscious about my facial anomaly. As a child, I never realized I was any different, but as an adult, my syndrome is sometimes all I notice. I morphed from a young girl who never felt an ounce different than her peers into a woman who let her insecurities hinder her attempts at living a normal life. But my past is my past. By telling my story, I release any self-doubt I once harbored.

I'm not sure what's next for me. The future is something I'll never really be able to predict. Will I have more operations? I suppose, if they're necessary, yes. Will I have even more nightmares? Without a doubt. Will I let those nightmares define who I become? Absolutely not. Nothing in the world will break my spirit.

Who I am is a strong, independent woman, and nothing can change that. My Treacher Collins syndrome may have led me down some rocky roads through the years, but I am who I am because of everything I have gone through. It's time now for me to accept myself completely and without reservations. I can no longer allow my negative thoughts to hold me back.

I am finished making excuses about why my path in life isn't following the same trajectory as everyone else's. I am finally ready to work through my self-confidence issues and become the person I always knew I could be; the person my family and friends already see every single day. It won't be easy to disregard a lifetime of insecurities, but I know I have to try. This is my life. I control it. My past may be unchangeable, but my future is unlimited if I find the courage to accept myself as I am. It is time to look beyond the imperfections.

It is time for me to recognize that I am more than just a beautiful disaster. I am beautiful.

ABOUT THE AUTHOR

Kristin Bartzokis's life was defined the moment Kristin entered the world. When you're born with a facial abnormality such as Treacher Collins Syndrome, you're not the smart one, the funny one, or the pretty one; you're the girl with the strange face and hearing aid. This made Kristin a warrior from a young age. She surpassed boundaries and crashed through walls, proudly accepting the challenge to stand out. Kristin resides in Central Florida and works in product development for a local attraction. Once a champion gymnast, she now focuses on running marathons. In her free time, Kristin can be found designing T-shirts, watching baseball, searching for her next big adventure, and blogging at diaryofabeautifuldisaster.com.